W9-AXB-371

Workshop Mastery with Jimmy DiResta

A Guide to Working with Metal, Wood, Plastic, and Leather

DISCARD

Jimmy DiResta and John Baichtal
Foreword by Nick Offerman

SAN FRANCISCO, CA

Workshop Mastery with Jimmy DiResta

by Jimmy DiResta, Nick Offerman, and John Baichtal

Copyright © 2016 Maker Media. All rights reserved.

Printed in Canada.

Published by Maker Media, Inc., 1160 Battery Street East, Suite 125, San Francisco, CA 94111.

Maker Media books may be purchased for educational, business, or sales promotional use. Online editions are also available for most titles (*http://safaribooksonline.com*). For more information, contact O'Reilly Media's institutional sales department: 800-998-9938 or *corporate@oreilly.com*.

Editor: Roger Stewart
Production Editor: Nicholas Adams
Copyeditor: Amanda Kersey
Proofreader: Rachel Monaghan

Indexer: Ellen Troutman-Zaig
Interior Designer: David Futato
Cover Designer: Karen Montgomery
Illustrator: Rebecca Demarest

October 2016:   First Edition

Revision History for the First Edition

2016-09-22:   First Release

See *http://oreilly.com/catalog/errata.csp?isbn=9781457194030* for release details.

Make:, Maker Shed, and Maker Faire are registered trademarks of Maker Media, Inc. The Maker Media logo is a trademark of Maker Media, Inc. *Workshop Mastery with Jimmy DiResta* and related trade dress are trademarks of Maker Media, Inc.

Many of the designations used by manufacturers and sellers to distinguish their products are claimed as trademarks. Where those designations appear in this book, and Maker Media, Inc. was aware of a trademark claim, the designations have been printed in caps or initial caps.

While every precaution has been taken in the preparation of this book, the publisher and authors assume no responsibility for errors or omissions, or for damages resulting from the use of the information contained herein.

978-1-457-19403-0

[TI]

Table of Contents

Foreword

The term "mastery" gets thrown around an awful lot these days when it comes to people who can make things. Our consumerist society has grown very soft in some ways because people can exist comfortably without ever learning to use a screwdriver, let alone a lathe. These folks, who have chosen to live very comfortable lives requiring no skills beyond shopping online and occasionally walking to the john, are therefore understandably impressed when they see an actual human being melt paraffin wax, pour it into a mold with a wick, and then after it cools, pop out the finished candle. "Why, that person must be a candle master!" When people erroneously attempt to lay such a label on me, having seen a simple table or canoe paddle created with my hands and my woodworking tools, I quickly correct them: "No, I can assure you that I am not to be called a master. For you see, I know Jimmy DiResta."

Jimmy's superpowers are those of a sculptor combined with a handyman with an inventor with a blacksmith with a woodworker with a teacher with you-name-it. He's the love-child of Robin Hood and DaVinci and John Henry, wielding a sweetheart's demeanor that dozens of his Lower East Side neighbors will eagerly tell you about, since he's built something for damn near all of them over the years. Some pay, some just give him donuts.

I have known Jimmy for nine years now, and from the first visit to the last, I have learned something from him every time. His talent is more like a sickness. He can't stop making things from every possible material, and some seemingly impossible ones—metal, wood, glass, stone, resin, leather, paper—ad infinitum. Not only must he make things as completely as he can, always with an expedience that is steady and un-harried, but he also must teach us all about how he does it.

This urge manifested itself in a few different television shows over the years (*Dirty Money*, *Makin' It*, *Lord of the Fleas*), but as is the case with many bright talents, TV did not get along with Jimmy. I have experienced this clash myself. When the artist or the "talent" wants to work in a way that allows his gifts to fully flourish, but the TV company doesn't care so much about that fulfillment as much as churning out remunerative 22-minute packages of entertainment, the two factions will ultimately not see eye to eye. Imagine making a bench in your shop and a producer is standing there telling you to "speed it up" to make the edit of the show quicker.

Jimmy has been making videos of his work and posting them online for many years now, and he has found the perfect medium. YouTube allows him to operate his very own TV channel, as it were, and curious newcomers as well as devoted adherents flock to see his work in droves. He manipulates his video cameras, his editing equipment, his social media, and the World Wide Web with all the elan he brings to carving a heart from padauk wood. I never fail to be inspired by the results of Jimmy's most recent exploration. As long as he keeps learning, we lucky subscribers to all things DiResta will have the opportunity to follow him; and those of us with the good sense to sit in his classroom will be lucky indeed.

—*Nick Offerman*

Preface

Looking back on my career, I've encountered many different materials and have learned to use a bunch of tools unique to those materials. Because of this diversity I've mostly divided the chapters of this book by material. Let's go over the projects, tools, and techniques you'll encounter in the pages ahead:

Chapter 1, *The Making of a Maker*, introduces me and my background. I've worked on a lot of crazy projects over the years.

Chapter 2, *Woodshop Mastery*, expands your knowledge of woodworking tools and presents four cool projects that make use of those tools: a tool cabinet, a dovetail-joined bench, a toolbox made out of a pallet, and an electric guitar designed to look like an AK-47 assault rifle.

Chapter 3, *CNC Projects*, switches gears and talks about computer-numerically controlled (CNC) tools, specifically routers. I'll cover two projects I worked on involving these tools: a dart board enclosure and a wooden sign.

Chapter 4, *Working with Metal*, switches gears and covers the metal shop, and I'll comment on the various tools I use for my projects. Then I'll introduce you to four very different metalworking projects: a box sign cut on a band saw, a machete cut out of a saw blade, a wooden table with aluminum legs shaped on a lathe, and a skull belt buckle made out of cast metal.

Chapter 5, *Plastic Projects*, describes using styrene, one of my favorite materials with a lot of utility and flexibility. I also show how I built some styrene channel letters, and detail a chess set that I first machined on my lathe in brass, then cast in black and white resin.

Chapter 6, *Working with Leather*, focuses on the tools and practices of a leatherworker. I show you how I made a sheath for a big knife I forged as well as a leather backpack.

Chapter 7, *Building Your Own Tools*, concludes the book the best way possible, by describing my love affair with tools. I love playing with tools: using them, of course, but also restoring them and modifying them. I'll share a number of my favorite tool modifications, then describe five projects showing different approaches toward tool building. The first project shows how to add an aluminum handle to a double-bitted antique axe. I follow that with a lathe-turned mallet, a metal locket with functional keys attached to it, a brass-ringed wooden mallet, and an ice pick that I mass-produced for my online store.

Safari® Books Online

 *Safari Books Online* is an on-demand digital library that delivers expert content in both book and video format from the world's leading authors in technology and business.

Technology professionals, software developers, web designers, and business and creative professionals use Safari Books Online as their primary resource for research, problem solving, learning, and certification training.

Safari Books Online offers a range of plans and pricing for enterprise, government, education, and individuals.

Members have access to thousands of books, training videos, and prepublication manuscripts in one fully searchable database from publishers like Maker Media, O'Reilly Media, Prentice Hall Professional, Addison-Wesley Professional, Microsoft Press, Sams, Que, Peachpit Press, Focal Press, Cisco Press, John Wiley & Sons, Syngress, Morgan Kaufmann, IBM Redbooks, Packt, Adobe Press, FT Press, Apress, Manning, New Riders, McGraw-Hill, Jones & Bartlett, Course Technology, and hundreds more. For more information about Safari Books Online, please visit us online.

How to Contact Us

Please address comments and questions concerning this book to the publisher:

Maker Media, Inc.
1160 Battery Street East, Suite 125
San Francisco, CA 94111
877-306-6253 (in the United States or Canada)
707-639-1355 (international or local)

Maker Media unites, inspires, informs, and entertains a growing community of resourceful people who undertake amazing projects in their backyards, basements, and garages. Maker Media celebrates your right to tweak, hack, and bend any Technology to your will. The Maker Media audience continues to be a growing culture and community that believes in bettering ourselves, our environment, our educational system—our entire world. This is much more than an audience, it's a worldwide movement that Maker Media is leading. We call it the Maker Movement.

For more information about Maker Media, visit us online:

Make: and Makezine.com: makezine.com
Maker Faire: makerfaire.com
Maker Shed: makershed.com

To comment or ask technical questions about this book, send email to *bookquestions@oreilly.com*.

Acknowledgments

Jimmy DiResta: To my father, Joe DiResta, for giving me tools at a young age, and my mother, Eileen DiResta, for giving me patience to learn how to use them.

John Baichtal: The lion's share of thanks goes to Jimmy. I enjoyed working on the book with you and learned a ton. Let's do another one! Special thanks go to Brian Jepson and Roger Stewart for making this book possible. Finally, thanks beyond words go to my wife Elise, mom Barbara, mother-in-law Barbara, and kids Arden, Rose, and Jack for having continually encouraged and inspired me over the years.

The Making of a Maker

I'm Jimmy DiResta and I've been making things my entire life, literally since I was old enough to stand in front of a saw. When I was a little kid my dad kept putting tools in front of me, my brothers, and my sister. I had the most curiosity about how tools worked and my dad kept nurturing it. He put me in front of a saw and I stuck my thumb in it right away. In the beginning I'd get cut here and there, and I still get cut once in a while.

Growing Up DiResta

I basically grew up in a workshop environment. Some kids see something they want and wish they could buy; I just went and built it. I wanted a crossbow, so I made one. The trigger mechanism was a challenge to figure out. I tried a bunch of different mechanisms until I perfected it. While most kids want to play basketball, I was developing a dart gun that would puncture the skin of the ball.

Making a mechanism like this requires thousands of tiny decisions, and trial and error experimenting with the spring tension in the trigger, or the strength of the projectile bow or rubber band. I learned things in this process that I still think of and use daily. As a kid I was not aware of the lessons I was learning.

I worked at a sign shop in high school, starting as a helper. At home I would cut letters on my band saw. One day I proved I was good enough to cut letters on their band saw. Eventually I would sit most of the day cutting all the letters for all the signs. I was 18 at the time; the next best-skilled guy was 50. Thirty years later, I use a CNC machine to cut most of my signage.

About a year after high school, I met a friend who was going to the School of Visual Arts. He encouraged me to check it out. I started going to SVA for graphic design, but pretty soon I realized all of my solutions were three-dimensional. I was making things and shooting them with a camera, and that was my graphic design solution. I switched to the 3D Illustration program, which was a much better fit.

Just when I was about to graduate, I took an elective called Toys and Invention. I've always been a person with a lot of creative ideas, and the teacher encouraged me to be an inventor.

Toy Building

From 1990 through around 2008, I designed toys. I have about 25 patents in the toy business. Most of them involve slime and other gross things kids love. You can see an example in Figure 1-1, the drawing for US patent # 5846116, which is a hollow rubber baby dinosaur. It comes in an egg that kids squeeze to make a gurgling noise.

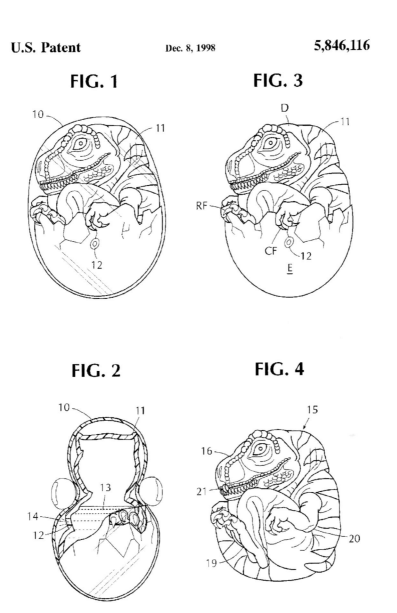

Figure 1-1 *What's not to like about a toy baby dinosaur?*

Another of my creations is Gurglin' Gutz (Figure 1-2), which consists of simulated brains, hearts, and so forth, inside a plastic sphere of colored slime. You squeeze it to make gross noises.

Figure 1-2 *As a toymaker I specialized in gross-out toys like Gurglin' Gutz*

While I enjoyed designing toys, I had some freelance projects I worked on. One of the most fun was modifying electric guitars.

Guitar Making

About the same time I started making toys, a friend introduced me to the owners of a guitar shop. I made a few guitars for them. One of the owners knew guitarist Steve Vai, and I ended up making my first celebrity guitar for him—the flaming skull design you can see in Figure 1-3.

Figure 1-3 *I built this guitar for Steve Vai*

Steve played it on David Letterman the same day I gave it to him. It was 1990, I was out of school for five months, and I felt like a pro! My girlfriend was working at a store as the register girl. There was a rock and roll guy that would flirt with her. She told him about me and that I made guitars, and she showed him the photo of the Steve Vai guitar. He had seen it the night before on the Letterman show and immediately wanted to meet me. His name was Adam Holland. He was a professional guitarist and had an endorsement deal with ESP guitars. So I began to make him a few guitars, developed a relationship with ESP, and added a few nice pieces to my portfolio.

At this time I was working on a bunch of projects, gaining experience, and developing a foundation to one day be able to raise my day rate. I still take jobs for free to learn new things. I do this to keep my problem-solving skills sharp and in tune. When I first purchased my CNC router last year, I needed to learn how to use it on real jobs. I made anything my clients needed simply to use and learn the software. Staying humble and looking for the lesson in any situation always helps me.

Making Television

My brother is a former NYC transit cop who did standup comedy. He did a one-person show that got turned into a television series and moved to L.A. A few years later he was between shows and asked me if I could film him picking through the trash and making a table from what he found. It was 2002, and I had been experimenting with video editing using Final Cut. So I went out to record him and put together a seven-minute tape for a show called *Trash to Cash*.

His agent was pleasantly surprised that the tape and edit were actually good. Because of the tape, we got a meeting at FX Networks. I put together a presentation of ideas for a full TV season. I was hoping to get a job on the show as a behind-the-scenes designer/producer. I had my portfolio with me and a big book of ideas: hand-sketched and Photoshopped images of various ideas for episodes. The producer we met with at FX asked me if I wanted to be on camera, which was very unexpected. I said yes, of course—he liked the idea of me being the "designer" brother and John being the "funny" brother. We ended up shooting seven episodes, including one where I pimped out an old caddy (Figure 1-4) with crushed blue velvet, carpeting, and gold-painted detailing.

Figure 1-4 *Making "Trash to Cash" restoring this sweet old car*

We went on to make a show called *Hammered.* We made the pitch tape on our own without any network or production company. My friend was a hairdresser; one of her clients was a network executive at HGTV. She told her friend about me. I sent in a tape…and 12 months later *Hammered* was being made for HGTV. It aired 28 episodes in '06–07. I made another guitar for this show—a guitar with flames carved into it; you can see it in

Figure 1-5. You could see preliminaries in my woodshop videos, showing the way the project came together, which involved a lot of planning and sketching before I touched a tool.

Figure 1-5 *The flaming guitar I built for "Hammered"*

Another popular build from the show was a classic doghouse (Figure 1-6) made from scraps found in an actual junkyard.

Figure 1-6 *A junkyard doghouse fit for a junkyard dog*

In 2010, a friend asked me to visit him at the new production company where he was working. They needed new signage, and I agreed to make it for them. While there, I asked if they took submissions for ideas. I sent my friend the YouTube link for *Lord of the Fleas*, an idea for a show I had shot in 2004 but which had never come to anything.

Lord of the Fleas is about finding trash and reworking it for sale at the flea market. Everyone loved the tape, but no deal came of it. So I just put it on my YouTube channel. It was getting some hits; a few people loved the idea, but it still was not getting any traction.

The owner of the production company called me one evening and asked if he could show it around. He showed it to Discovery Channel that week. Ten months later we were in production. Discovery aired the show with a new title, *Dirty Money.* In the summer of 2011 we aired one season.

One of the notable builds from the show was a gramophone restoration (Figure 1-7).

Figure 1-7 *This gramophone now sports a restored trumpet*

Another of the projects, a set of wrench pulls (Figure 1-8) harkens back to a favorite category of projects: modifying tools, restoring them, and repurposing them in unexpected ways. You'll get to see a lot of modified tools in this book!

Figure 1-8 *These drawer pulls are fashioned from junked wrenches*

Another fun project was a prop replica, the signature bike from *Pee Wee's Big Adventure*, seen in Figure 1-9.

Figure 1-9 *I restored this bike and made it look like Pee Wee's bicycle from the movie*

Although it doesn't sound like it, I never was able to get much traction in the TV business. People ask why I'm not working on another show. It's not because I'm not interested. It's because *they're* not interested.

In the meantime I've found something better: making my own shows and posting them on YouTube.

Uploading My Own

I started putting up YouTube videos in 2012. There was a guy who got two million hits with a video of his truck running. I put up a video of my truck running and it didn't get any hits. At first I developed my channel as a way of attracting viewers for my next TV project, but eventually I stopped caring about TV and focused on the shows for their own sake. I recorded myself building projects, mostly sped up and without subtitles or narration.

After about 15 videos, Make: noticed and asked me to do some videos for them. It's been three years now, and I've done over 80 videos for them. My Make: videos include some fan favorites, like "Ice Pick 2.0," "Birch Slice Table" (seen in Figure 1-10), and the "Pallet Toolbox." (You'll find the latter in the pages of this book.) I've done tool restorations, furniture and sign projects for clients, as well as storage and tools for my own use here in the shop.

Figure 1-10 *I've done a bunch of videos for Make:*

The most important thing about YouTube is being able to talk directly to my fans, without the filter of a TV station or production company in between. Sometimes it's a bad sort of communication, with nitpickers disagreeing with my techniques or wringing their hands over some customization I made to a tool.

Most of the fans I have dealt with, however, have been excited, supportive, eager to learn, and happy to watch my videos purely as a source of inspiration. People sometimes ask why I don't explain things in more detail. The answer is, I've never intended my videos to be exact how-tos. I don't like to be preachy about what I do. The making experience is totally personal. I'm not trying to teach you the *right* way to use a band saw or hold a drill. I'm just trying to inspire you to try it yourself.

Welcome to my workshop!

Woodshop Mastery

2

My first and greatest love as a maker has always been working with wood. As long as I can remember I've stood in front of band saws and drill presses. I've created a lot of very fun projects, but also numerous practical and useful projects.

You can see both kinds of projects in this chapter. I'll share four cool items I built in my woodshop, beginning with a large set of oak and mahogany tool drawers, then moving on to a dovetailed bench I created out of a massive piece of hardwood. From this practical and large-scale beginning I move on to two more whimsical projects. I describe transforming an ordinary shipping pallet into a toolbox, carefully extracting the boards from the pallet so as not to damage them, then trimming and planing them into usable material. The final project of the chapter, the Gattar (Figure 2-1) merges an electric guitar into an AK-47 to create a unique musical instrument.

Figure 2-1 *I'll show you how I built my Gattar, an electric guitar shaped like a rifle*

Before the projects, however, I'll cover some of my favorite tools, including much of the equipment I used to build these four projects.

Tools

I use these tools on a daily basis in my shop, and maybe they could be useful to you.

Chisel

I keep my chisels sharp and polished. I have a straight set as well as a set of sexy carving chisels. My dad bought the carving set when I was 11 years old, but I was too intimidated to use them until I was a teenager. Those are my good chisels. No one's allowed to touch them.

I use a piece of wood as the hammer. It's the cutout from a guitar I made in 1985. I kept it, and it's always been my tap hammer when I do carving. It's just a scrap of wood I picked up, and I've used it for 30 years.

Compound Miter Saw

Sometimes called a chop saw, a sliding compound miter saw is a circular saw that can be chopped down at materials, but can also be pulled back more than a foot to cut wider lengths of wood like a radial arm saw. You can cut bevels, angles, and compound bevels. I use a DeWalt 12" saw, seen in Figure 2-2, and it runs about $600.

Figure 2-2 *The compound miter saw makes precise cuts in smaller pieces of wood*

Cordless Drill

I keep a bunch of cordless drills around. I organize them in sets of two: one regular drill with high and low speeds, as well as a hammering action for drilling into masonry. For driving screws I use a 20 V cordless impact driver, and it accepts standard-sized hex bits.

I feel like the technology is such that pretty much any cordless drill is just as good as any other. People ask me which drill to buy, and I tell them to choose the one that's their favorite color.

Drill bits

I use a variety of bits in my work:

Standard

> I have tons of partial sets of standard bits lying around. It's just cheaper to buy a new set than purchase individual bits. Sets are divided into good and bad sets. A good set is one that has all the bits, and I can bring it to a job site with the expectation that there will be none missing.

Countersinks

> These bore a wider hole around the main one, so the screws can be set flush against the surface of the material. I always have a jar of countersinks handy.

Step bits

> Used for drilling wider holes in sheet metal. I bring a package of these to every job site.

Forstner bits

> My clean set of Forstner bits is labeled DO NOT USE, and that applies to everyone in the shop but me. Of all the methods I've tried, these bits are the best for cutting big holes in wood.

Spade bits

> Another way of making a big hole is a spade bit, which I keep around but almost never use. The holes they make are just too rough, and I mostly use them for sheetrock.

Festool Domino Joiner

This system makes the process of connecting two pieces of wood together with pegs very quick, very sure, and totally repeatable. You simply press the machine into the material and it carves out mortises that precisely match the tenons you buy with the machine. I generally don't buy Festool because it's expensive; this tool is around $950. However, it was a gift from my girlfriend, and it really has improved my workflow.

Dust Collection System

I use a couple of different methods to keep dust in my shop at a minimum. My Harbor Freight system (seen in Figure 2-3) is primarily connected to the back of my table saw, which is the main thing in the shop that generates a lot of dust.

I also use a couple of smaller, portable dust systems, which essentially consist of shop vacs that you can hook up to your tool. For instance, my palm sander has a dedicated hose that plugs into the back of the tool. I use these around the shop when it would be too inconvenient to use the main collector.

Figure 2-3 *My Harbor Freight dust collection system mostly cleans up after my table saw*

Hammers

I keep a variety of hammers on hand, depending on what I'm trying to hammer. I have regular and small-sized steel hammers, ones with brass and lead heads for working with softer materials that might be damaged by steel, as well as even softer ones like rubber, leather, and wood mallets.

Planer

I bought the Delta planer in Figure 2-4 brand new, maybe in 1990. I've changed the blades a bunch of times over the years, and along the way learned not to put timbers I found on the street through this tool without inspecting them first. I've passed 3×10 beams through this thing, and they're all full of concrete dust and basically ruin the blade immediately.

In storage I have a Rigid planer and a DeWalt planer, and they all work pretty much the same and have the same amount of snipe. This is where the beginning or end of the board gets pinched as it runs through the planer. I solve this by pushing the main board through with a sacrificial board of the same thickness.

Figure 2-4 *The Delta planer smooths down pieces of wood*

Router

These rotary tools carve away material using bits that look a lot like drill bits. I keep a compact DeWalt router in the shop. It's a 1.25 HP, which is strong enough for most uses. When that's not the case, I have a heavier DeWalt that packs 2.25 HP and includes a built-in dust collector that sucks up most of the sawdust generated by this tool.

Router bits

Popular types of bits include straight, dado, rabetting, flush trim, and dovetail, and I try to keep a wide variety around. I have a huge drawer of router bits that I got from around three shop buyouts. People ask me how I organize my router bits and I send them a picture of my drawer. It's not a rock tumbler—the bits don't move around much in the drawer. I keep a second drawer with the router's wrenches and other attachments, plus I include a handful of bits that are currently my sharpest and best of each type. After so many systems and boards with holes in them, this is the system for me.

Pneumatic Brad Nailer

I use these nailers all the time for keeping things in place when I'm gluing up. I use both small 23-gauge nailers as well as larger-sized 18-gauge ones. They're so easy to pop a nail in at a moment's notice. People ask what are the best brands, and Porter Cable and Bostich seem to be the ones that don't break.

Hand Saws

My go-to is a little crosscut saw I got from Lee Valley. I keep the blade free of rust and the blade-guard on, so it has stayed the sharpest the longest of all my saws, and I use it for fine cutting. I keep a larger DeWalt saw around for rough stuff. I also keep one in the truck in case I spot a piece of lumber and don't want the whole thing.

I have an antique Disston hand saw from the 1950s. I liked the saw because of the history of it, and I bought it from an antique shop in Alabama. It turned out to be quite sharp, and I use it for fine cuts.

People always ask me, why do I hand saw stuff so much? One reason might be simply to stay in practice. Sometimes it's easier just grabbing a saw and making a few swipes than running an electrical cord.

I also use small dovetailing saws and get them from the Home Depot for 13 bucks. Whenever one of them gets dinged up, I just throw it in my junk drawer.

Sawzall

I have five of these reciprocating saws. It's the sort of thing people buy and never use and then ask me, "Hey, can you use this tool?" So I inherit a bunch of them. They're perfect for cutting apart pallets and rough work like cutting into a wall. However, I've found them to be useful for fine work in certain circumstances. For instance, I like to use a sawzall to finish a cut on a thing too thick for a table saw. I cut it on the top and bottom with the table saw, finish the cut with the sawzall, then clean up the cut so no one can tell.

SawStop Table Saw

I've used many different table saws over the years, but I really like my SawStop, the 3HP Professional unit seen in Figure 2-5. It's pretty heavy-duty and I can't stall it, no matter how hard I push wood through it.

It's got a 36" fence, which is great because I can cut pretty much anything. The most notable feature of the SawStop involves a safety mechanism that shuts down instantly if the blade is touched while spinning. Because of the physical needs of this brake, the arbor and bearings are much stronger and more durable that most table saws I've used.

Another clever feature consists of a two-part guard that flips over the blade, protecting you from flying wood chips while also marking the blade's height. It also has an attachment to my dust collection system, so sawdust is hoovered away as I cut.

SawStop gave me this saw for free, and I thank them because I really like it.

Figure 2-5 *The SawStop table saw includes a touch-sensitive safety brake*

Hand Planes

These tools help smooth down areas of wood, prior to sanding. I use my Veritas shoulder plane for cheeks and tenons. However, my latest acquisition is a Lie-Nielsen Np. 610 low-angle jack rabbet plane. The blade goes to the very edge of the plane, allowing me to get down into corners with it. My go-to hand plane is the low-angle block plane from Veritas.

Glues

Wood Glue
> I mostly use yellow carpenter's glue repackaged into small squeeze bottles I get from the restaurant supply store down the block. The bottles I get from the glue company usually aren't very usable. Brandwise I prefer Titebond, but I've often used cheaper brands with great success.

3M Spray Glue
> I use this spray glue all the time. I like the #77 because it has a lower tack than #90. This has some unexpected uses. For instance, I'll spray-glue a stack of MDF together and run it through the band saw, and then break it apart. With the #90 it wouldn't come apart afterwards!

2p10 Glue
> This is a cyanoacrylate glue, also known as CA glue, and it comes with an activator spray.

PVA Glue

> This stuff is used for bookbinding; I use it for gluing leather to wood. Elmer's glue will get hard and chippy, but PVA stays rubbery and flexible.

West System Epoxy

> I found out about this stuff from friends who build boats. It leaves a nice hard-shell finish and also fills up cracks. West System also sells sawdust-like fillers that allow you to change the color, texture, and finish of the epoxy.

Veritas Mk. II Power Sharpening System

You can get your plane blades nice and sharp using the Mk. II sharpening system. It consists of a 650-RPM turntable and a blade holder that can be set to 5-degree increments, allowing you to perfectly hone an edge in a matter of minutes.

Summary

I hope you found my selection of tools helpful in stocking your own workbench. Next, I'll share this chapter's projects.

Organizing with Oak and Mahogany Tool Drawers

It amazes me sometimes how many *really tiny* tools I collect. I'm always picking up bits and blades of various types, whether at garage sales or flea markets. I acquire still more tools when I buy a machine, as it usually comes with all sorts of attachments. A case in point is my Bridgeport milling machine, a giant tool I keep in my workshop in upstate New York. It comes with about a million bits, so I need a set of tool drawers to organize them. I came up with the simple-seeming set of drawers seen in Figure 2-6.

Figure 2-6 *I built a set of drawers to store drill bits and other small tools*

Tools and Parts to Build the Drawers

I used the following when building my drawers:

- Table saw
- Dado bit
- Chop saw
- Router
- Cordless drill
- Brad nailer
- Planer
- Lead hammer
- Sandpaper
- Wood glue

Building Steps

Here are the steps I followed to build my drawers:

1. Cut the horizontal dividers

I began by cutting up a bunch of plywood on my table saw. I'm not even sure how much plywood this particular project used, but it was a lot! I then took the first set of boards to my chop saw and cut them down. These sections will serve as horizontal dividers between the sets of drawers.

Next, I took these dividers and cut dados into them. Dados are trenches that hold other pieces of wood. I cut dados not just for the sides of the cabinet, but also interior grooves for the vertical dividers that will hold the drawers. The top and bottom dividers were one-sided, and the rest were two-sided.

I used hold-down clamps (seen in Figure 2-7) to secure the boards to my sled, which keep the wood in place for accurate cuts. I cut the grooves with the help of a stacked dado set, essentially several saw blades stacked up to make a very wide cut. I'd make one cut, then move over the board six inches at a time. I used a stopper strip to create even six-inch spacing between dados. I kind of made up my own procedure. I had never seen anyone make a set of drawers like this before and wasn't sure how to begin, so I sat down and figured out how it would be done. As a final step on the horizontal dividers, I used the chop saw to cut the boards down to the perfect size.

Figure 2-7 *Cutting the dados with the help of the saw's sled*

2. Cut the vertical dividers

I began cutting 6″ × 16″ strips of plywood for the vertical dividers. I cut off strips of scrap wood, then cut them down to size on the chop saw. They're all the same size, so I just made a bunch of them!

3. Build stages

After I cut the horizontal and vertical dividers, it was time to build each stage. By that I mean a horizontal divider with all five vertical dividers glued in place. I grabbed the first board and put wood glue in the dados, added the dividers, then secured them with a brad nailer.

Once I had a section done, I set it aside and built another to give the first one time to tack up. The glue is doing most of the holding; the nails just keep it in place. I was careful to wipe up the glue, not because I didn't need the staying power, but so the globs didn't take up space and prevent the drawers from sliding in and out.

When I had two, I glued them together with dividers, then clamped them together and let them dry. The most important thing is to make sure everything stays straight. I wouldn't want all these little channels to become crooked.

4. Assemble the cabinet

As each set of stages was completed, I glued it to the next with more dividers. I assembled the basic cabinet out of the stacks of sections. The most important consideration at this point is to keep everything straight and level. I checked and rechecked everything, then clamped it down to dry overnight.

Note that the lower levels have only two drawers (as seen in Figure 2-8), each twice as big as the others. I didn't bother doing the dados any different for these stages, as you won't be able to see the extra cuts when the drawers are in.

Once the cabinet was dry I put the back on; it's just a sheet of plywood. I'd already cut it to fit so it was pretty close. First I glued the backs of all of the boards and then nailed the sheet of plywood nailed in my brad nailer. I let it sit overnight.

Figure 2-8 *Measuring diagonally to ensure the cabinet isn't crooked*

5. Add the veneer

The next day I began adding the veneer. Because the sides clearly show the edges of all the horizontal dividers, I added a cosmetic veneer of quarter-inch oak plywood over it.

I glued the sides with wood glue and added the plywood, shown in Figure 2-9. I tacked it down with my brad nailer, using some pin nails to keep it in place until the glue dried. I trimmed off the excess with a flush cutter.

Figure 2-9 *Gluing on a veneer of plywood*

I added the top piece of veneering, gluing the plywood and then applying the veneering, the same way I did with the sides. I also glued a small piece of hardwood on the corners (Figure 2-10), concealing the edges of the veneering. I taped it into place with blue painter's tape.

Figure 2-10 *Gluing in a cosmetic strip of hardwood*

6. Cut the edge banding

I cut small strips of mahogany on my table saw. These will make the plywood edges of the front of the cabinet look prettier. I glued the strips onto the front of the cabinet, on the spaces between the drawers. Those plywood edges were pretty functional, so the mahogany dressed it up considerably.

The vertical stripes I affixed first, then cut off the excess. The spaces between them needed a little more care, so I cut them precisely to size on the chop saw, then glued them in place and taped them with painter's tape.

Once the glue was dry, I sanded them with a long board covered in sandpaper. I used the board because there are so many openings and having a longer sanding implement helped to bridge those gaps. I also tried using a 12" sanding disk on a stick, with a big steel weight to give it more authority.

7. Cut the drawer parts

I cut strips of oak on the table saw and then used my chop saw to cut them down. These pieces will be the faces of the drawers. I used a block of wood to make sure they were all the same width.

Next, I made the drawer sides using a piece of ash I had. Someone had given me some thin strips of ash. They were a little cupped, but I knew that for the small pieces of wood I'd need, it wouldn't matter. I cut the boards down, trimming both sides to keep them smooth.

Next, I cut a big sheet of half-inch oak plywood down using my table saw, making long strips that will serve as the bottoms of the drawers. Once again, I used the chop saw to cut the boards to size.

8. Assemble the drawers

The next step involved assembling the drawers out of the boards I just cut. I used a router to round the edge of the faces, just to give them a little bevel.

Then I cut a rabbet (Figure 2-11) around the edges with a dado blade on my table saw. These will help the face inset into the front of the cabinet. I cut a quarter-inch around the edge, but double-cut the bottom to half an inch, because the drawers' bottom is thicker than the sides.

Figure 2-11 *Cutting rabbets in the drawer faces*

Finally, I assembled the drawers with the usual wood glue and brad nailer. Figure 2-12 shows a completed drawer getting a quick planing.

Figure 2-12 *Planing and sanding a completed drawer*

While I worked, I basically used the cabinet as my file (Figure 2-13) to keep each one of the drawer parts in its place. When I was ready to build a drawer, I'd get the parts out of the cubby and put the finished drawer back in.

Figure 2-13 *Keeping the drawer parts organized*

9. Make the base

The cabinet needs a base, because even without the tools in the drawers, it weighs a couple hundred pounds. I cut and planed some mahogany boards, and these will make up the base's construction. The base's legs consist of pairs of mahogany boards glued together.

Next, I used a domino jig (seen in Figure 2-14) to cut peg holes in the mahogany pieces. This kind of joinery is called mortise and tenon, and it's very strong. When had mortised all of the holes, I used tenons and a lead hammer to bang it all together with glue.

Figure 2-14 *Using a domino jig to drill mortises into the mahogany*

I clamped the base, using shims and extra tenons as pads so the clamps didn't dent the mahogany. Before I left the base to dry overnight, I added poplar strips to the inside with the air nailer. The strips will attach the base to the cabinet.

I screwed the base to the cabinet (Figure 2-15) using poplar strips to attach the two together. Knowing that the cabinet would get pushed around a bit, I added big glides to the bottom of the legs. I'd recycled them from a piece of furniture I'd found on the street.

Figure 2-15 *Attaching the base to the cabinet*

10. Finish the cabinet

With the drawers and cabinet done, it was time to add the finishing touches. I painted the drawer fronts and mahogony trim with paint, and hit the veneered sides and top as well. However, I didn't bother painting the back, because no one will see it.

I put a drawer pull on each face, using a little jig to ensure they're straight and centered. They're vintage-looking plates (seen in Figure 2-16) and also contain a slot for a small label, which will be helpful when I start putting parts in the drawers.

Figure 2-16 *I made a jig to ensure the drawer pulls were centered*

Finally, I used Briwax to lubricate the sides of the drawers and to keep them free of dirty fingerprints. Next up, I just have to label it and fill it with junk!

Summary

I had mixed feelings about this project. On one hand it filled a need I had: a storage cabinet able to accommodate my huge collection of drill bits and Bridgeport parts I'd acquired over the years. On the other hand, it was kind of repetitive, with tons of identical cuts and countless pieces of wood to keep track of. Now that it's done, however, I can safely say that I'm proud of my work!

Dovetailing a Massive Oak Bench

I really don't cut dovetails that often. It's odd because it's not an unusual way of connecting two pieces of wood. In fact, it's been around since before writing was invented. It simply wasn't a type of joinery I practiced very often.

When I decided on this project—which was right after I saw the board that would be used in it—I knew I'd want something without a lot of excess detail. I was visualizing a bench that was monolithic and strong, but also simple and elegant.

I decided on using dovetail joints because it was a very strong and durable method to combine two pieces of wood, but also didn't involve a lot of extra hardware. You can see what I came up with in Figure 2-17.

Figure 2-17 *Pitch-black oak melded with steel make for a truly massive bench*

Tools and Materials Used

Mostly I used a variety of saws to make this bench. Dovetailing is a technique that predates the pyramids, and as such it doesn't need a lot of tools. This is what I used:

- Table saw
- Hand saw

- Dovetailing saw
- Dremel cutout tool
- Hammer and chisel
- Rigid milling machine
- Chopping band saw
- Huge piece of oak!
- Steel stock
- Presto black gel
- WD Lockwood dye
- Ebony Briwax

Building the Bench

I got a huge oak plank from a sawmill down the road from my house in upstate New York. It's 9' long by 16" wide and 2.5" thick, and weighs around 200 pounds. It was $50. From the moment I saw the board I knew I was going to do this very project. Here are the steps I took to build it:

1. Cut down the wood

I cut off the ends of the board, trimming off the S-hooks. These pieces of metal (seen in Figure 2-18) keep the wood from splitting and warping, but won't be needed anymore.

In addition, I needed to fit the board into the truck for the ride home, so I cut 18" lengths off to serve as legs.

I decided not to plane it flat, because I wanted to keep the rough saw marks from when it was first milled.

Figure 2-18 *Cutting off the S-hooks*

2. Cut dovetails in the first leg

I drew 60-degree dovetails on one of the legs using an angle finder. Once I'd identified the waste wood, I marked it boldly in Sharpie (Figure 2-19) so I wouldn't accidentally cut out the wrong part—it happens!

Then I cut into the wood with the hand saw. I was careful to keep the angle perfect or the dovetails wouldn't work.

Figure 2-19 *Cutting the first dovetail*

Once the side cuts had been made, I dug into the waste wood with a Dremel cutout tool. It only cut partway through, so I cleared the last bits with a chisel and dovetailing saw.

3. Cut dovetails in the top

Having one set of dovetails, I was ready to make the matching set in the top of the bench. I put the leg next to the top, approximately how they would be when nested. I marked the edge of the bench's top.

Then I marked the top of the bench corresponding with the dovetails I cut into the leg. I made a rubbing of the cross sections (Figure 2-20) and spray-glued it to the top.

Figure 2-20 *A traced template tells me where to saw*

I used a chisel to cut into the traced lines in order to give my hand saw a clearer cutting path for me to follow.

When I had a nice big groove, I went to work with my hand saw. The wood had a tendency to grab the blade, so I waxed it periodically with Minwax, and that really helped.

After I got the dovetails cleaned up, I did a test fit. The two pieces (seen in Figure 2-21) came together perfectly, which is great because this was the first set of dovetails I'd done in many years, and only the third set I've done in my life.

Figure 2-21 *A test fit confirmed the dovetails were cut right*

4. Cut the other set of dovetails

With that success under my belt, I replicated the dovetails on the other side, using my hand saw, Dremel cutout tool, and chisel to basically do the same thing. For some reason this set was tighter than the first. I wasn't able to figure out why, but they came together without cracking, which is the important part.

5. Saw off excess material

With the legs seated, I went to work with a dovetailing saw to cut off the excess. Because of the aforementioned bowing of the wood, some of the dovetails were longer than others, so I trimmed them off with my saw (Figure 2-22) and then gave it a light sanding with my palm sander.

Figure 2-22 *Sawing off extra material*

6. Build the truss rod assembly

Next I began working on the truss rod that would help reinforce the bench. First, I cut off two 4" disks of steel stock using my Craftsman chopping band saw. These parts will serve as flanges on the bench.

After that I cut off about 6' of truss rod that will be supported by those flanges I just cut. Figure 2-23 shows the rod in the chopping band saw.

Figure 2-23 *Cutting off some steel rod*

I drilled holes in the center of the disks corresponding to the diameter of the truss rod. I used my Rigid milling machine, which doesn't get a lot of use. It's good for long, slow drills. After cutting the center holes I gave each truss a quick polish on the belt sander.

Then I drilled the mounting holes with the drill press, with countersink bits to help the brass screws fit flush.

Finally, I welded the flanges onto the truss rod, positioning them so there was about 3" of rod sticking out of either end. Figure 2-24 shows one of the trusses.

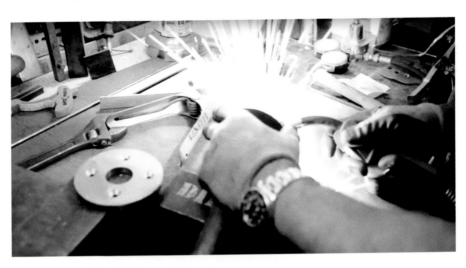

Figure 2-24 *Welding the flanges to the rod*

7. Install the truss rod

It was time to install the truss rod by trapping it between the bench's legs. I removed the legs with the help of a couple of small prybars.

I marked both legs where the truss rod would go, then drilled holes with the drill press.

Then I reassembled the bench with the truss rod in place, as seen in Figure 2-25. It's trapped between the legs, and once bolted into place, help keep the legs upright.

Figure 2-25 *Installing the truss rod that reinforces the bench*

Before I tapped the legs into place for the final time, I glued the dovetails. I used a pipe clamp to get them as tight as I possibly could.

Finally, I drilled pilot holes and screwed brass screws in to secure the flanges. Be careful with brass screws because you can easily strip them.

8. Finish the bench

The bench was done—all I needed to do was add a coat of dye and polish it up. I began with a few coats of WD Lockwood Dye, a wood dye that sinks right in without filling up the fibers. It's the best way to get pitch black oak.

The next day I gave it a light sanding and polished it with ebony Briwax, which colors as well as polishes. You can see the nearly completed bench in Figure 2-26. As a final step, I colored the steel with Presto black gel, making the entire bench a really great glossy black. It weighs around 150 pounds including the metal, making it extremely sturdy and stable.

Figure 2-26 *Applying ebony Briwax to bring out the shine*

Summary

I visualized this exact project the moment I laid eyes on the piece of lumber at the sawmill. Being able to execute my idea exactly as intended was very satisfying, and I'm proud of how the bench turned out.

Turn a Pallet into a Toolbox

I had been thinking of making a toolbox out of wood repurposed from an old pallet, and when I spotted just the perfect pallet right in front of the workshop, I said to myself, "You know, that's a pretty good-looking pallet" and picked it up.

Most pallets have skinny little strips of hard oak, and they're very brittle, but this one had thicker planks of pine, and I knew it would be useful. Follow along to learn how I built my toolbox—you can see the finished project in Figure 2-27.

Figure 2-27 *Learn how to build this handy toolbox out of waste wood*

Tools and Materials

The toolbox project used the following tools:

- Sawzall
- Delta planer
- Table saw
- Brad nailer
- Rubber mallet
- Disk sander

Building Steps

I performed the following steps to build my toolbox:

1. Break apart the pallet

The easiest way to take apart a pallet is literally to saw the nails in half—if you try to pry it apart, the boards will break. I ran a sawzall between the top planks and the side supports, slicing the nails with a hacksaw blade. After cutting as much as I could with the sawzall, I used a claw hammer and rubber hammer to pry apart the big pieces.

I removed the remaining nail heads by poking them through on one side, then using a hammer (Figure 2-28) to pull them out.

Figure 2-28 *Removing nail ends with a hammer*

2. Dress the boards

I ran the planks through the planer, smoothing down both sides while maintaining a uniform thickness. This is called "dressing" and will help make the toolbox a little more finished-looking.

Then I used a table saw to trim the widths, cutting out cracks and other damage whenever possible while trying to get the most yield out of each board.

When I had all the boards planed and trimmed, I repaired as many cracks as I could (Figure 2-29) by gluing and clamping them.

Figure 2-29 *Trimming the widths*

3. Cut the toolbox ends

I glued some of the boards together to form double-width planks, and they will form the broader sides and bottom of the toolbox. Figure 2-30 shows me gluing two boards together.

Figure 2-30 *Gluing narrow boards together to make a wide one*

Then I used the chop saw to cut shorter lengths of double-width board for the toolbox's ends. Then I adjusted the miter on my chop saw and cut the tapers. I stacked the boards so

I cut both sides simultaneously, keeping them even. Figure 2-31 shows me making the cuts.

Figure 2-31 *Cutting angles on the end pieces*

4. Cut the sides and bottom

Readjusting back to 90 degrees, I cut single-width boards for use as two of the box's sides. Then I cut another length of double-width board to form the bottom. You can see these parts in Figure 2-32.

Figure 2-32 *All the pieces of the toolbox arranged together*

5. Cut dovetails in the boards

I used a wooden wedge (seen in Figure 2-33) to angle the boards precisely for cutting dovetails on the table saw. I cut the angles using the table saw, then used the band saw to trim away the waste material.

Figure 2-33 *Cutting dovetails at an angle with the help of a wedge*

When I had one dovetail finished, I traced it to cut its mate. This allows me to ensure they fit together precisely.

I cut out the traced dovetails on the band saw. You can see the side panel in Figure 2-34.

Figure 2-34 *Cutting dovetails on the ends*

6. Cut the handle

I cut the toolbox's handle out of one of the single boards. I cut a curve that I had free-drawn on the board. I went only halfway along the board, however. I used the waste pieces from the first part to trace the curve on the remaining part of the board with a marker, giving me a quick, easy, and symmetrical curve.

Then I drilled the handle holes on the sides, beginning with a series of holes (seen in Figure 2-35) bored with a Forstner bit.

I used a chisel to clean up the holes. I'm making a mortise that will hold the handle.

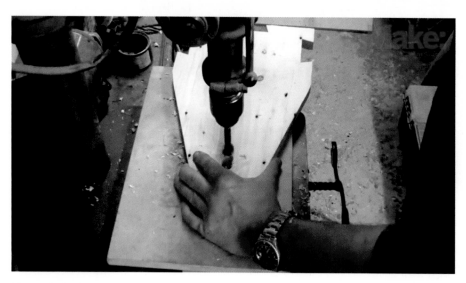

Figure 2-35 *Cutting holes for the handle*

7. Finish

I put the parts of the toolbox together without glue. I clamped the dovetails to ensure they were flush, then secured them in place with a couple of nails. Finally, I gave the toolbox a good sanding to smooth down any rough edges. The project is done!

Summary

This project definitely challenged me to make the most out of a notoriously unreliable medium: pallet wood. I'm really happy with how it turned out. Next, I'll describe the final project of the chapter, creating an electric guitar that looks like an AK-47.

Turning a Guitar into a Gattar

In the spring of 2013 my friend and former accountant was working with Wyclef Jean. Wyclef mentioned he wanted a signature guitar in the shape of a gun, because he wanted to illustrate the concept of turning guns into guitars. This was in response to the street violence in Chicago. My friend introduced us and we came up with an idea for a fully playable guitar shaped like an AK-47, gold just like Saddam Hussein's gold AK-47. Only a few hours from coming up with the concept, I was in the workshop putting it together. It's a very interesting project that came together in just a couple of days, and it's been my most successful video, getting me tons of recognition on YouTube. Figure 2-36 shows how the Gattar turned out.

Figure 2-36 *The Gattar is a fully playable electric guitar*

Tools and Materials

Beyond the big two, the guitar and the toy gun serving as a visual guide (visible in Figure 2-37), you'll need several tools and parts:

- Ibanez electric guitar
- Replica AK-47 (all plastic)
- Second electric guitar
- Band saw
- Dovetailing saw
- Router

Figure 2-37 *I needed to make the guitar look like the gun*

Building the Gattar

I took the following steps to build the Gattar:

1. Draw the design on the guitar

Using the replica gun as a guide, I free-handed the shape of the Gattar's body. I didn't know exactly how this project would come together, but I just dove right in, trusting my ability to overcome any problems that arose. However, I was pretty sure I knew I had to start with the main section of the guitar, including the neck. Figure 2-38 shows the design coming together.

Figure 2-38 *Drawing the gun shape on the guitar*

2. Remove the guitar's hardware

In order to reformulate the Ibanez as an AK-47 I needed to remove all of the guitar's electronics, because they'll interfere with cutting the new shape. That included stuff like knobs, wires, and the amp jack. I removed the metal plate from the back of the Ibanez, exposing the electronics.

3. Cut out the design

Having drawn the shape, I cut off the excess wood on my Delta band saw, seen in Figure 2-39.

Figure 2-39 *Cutting the guitar down to a gun shape. Just add the pistol grip!*

4. Shape the pistol grip's attachment point

I'll be adding both functional and cosmetic parts that will make the Gattar look like a gun. One of these is the pistol grip, and I carved away at the body with a dovetailing saw to create a small nub to which I'll eventually add a grip.

5. Cut out the stock and grip

I cut the stock out of a big chunk of walnut, as seen in Figure 2-40. I could have used a real gun's stock, but I didn't have one, and the dimensions I needed were different than the replica's stock. In any case, the replica is made out of flimsy plastic and would never hold up on tour.

Figure 2-40 *Cutting the stock and grip out of walnut*

After I had it cut out I ran it through the band saw some more, carving it into more of a natural, curved shape. I am most comfortable carving and sculpting on the band saw. I've been doing it so long, it's an easy way to quickly remove material. Holding the walnut in my hands and running it through the saw, I can slow down and see exactly where I'm at.

Next, I cut the pistol grip out of the walnut. Just as I did with the stock, I worked on the grip in the band saw (Figure 2-41) to round it a little more.

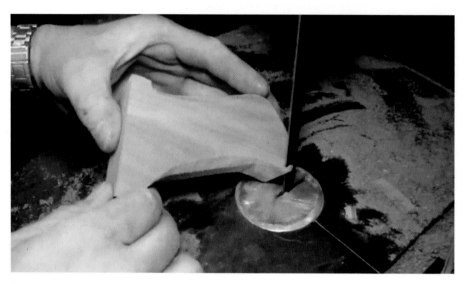

Figure 2-41 *Shaping the pistol grip*

6. Build the gas tube

Next I focused on a cosmetic part of the Gattar matching the AK-47's gas tube, which is found above the barrel with a wooden shroud covering it. Because this is a distinctive feature of the AK, I wanted to include it in the Gattar. I added some plastic I had lying around the shop, screwing it into the top of the guitar as shown in Figure 2-42.

After I had installed the plastic pole, I cut the wooden housing that covers the gas tube. This is so you don't burn your hand when the gun is firing. Of course, the Gattar doesn't need this, but it's nevertheless part of the AK-47's distinctive look.

Figure 2-42 *Attaching a piece of plastic on the top*

7. Make the banana clip mini guitar

The Gattar's magazine was a fun surprise to the project. It was Wyclef's idea. He really wanted the magazine to have its own little guitar pickups and strings! It was a little bizarre at first, but I said, "OK, let me see if I can figure it out." It ended up working out really well.

The first step was to cut out the banana shape. I made it out of an old cutting board I had lying around. Figure 2-43 shows me cutting the shape. Then I used a router to bevel the edges to look like the real magazine.

Figure 2-43 *Cutting the magazine shape out of a cutting board*

Then I used a Forstner bit on my drill press to cut out indents for the pickups and tuners.

Next, I installed the clip's bridges, pickups, and tuners, as seen in Figure 2-44. I ended up going out and buying another cheap guitar, and harvested the electronics out of it.

Then I strung the mini guitar. I'll take the strings off when I paint the instrument, but I'm putting them on early to test it out.

Figure 2-44 *Stringing the mini guitar*

As a final step for the mini guitar, I glued the banana clip onto the main body of the Gattar with five-minute epoxy, making sure to thread the pickups' wires through a hole for future access. I eventually added a couple of screws as well.

8. Finish attaching the gas tube

Having completed the delicate work on the banana clip, I finished up the cosmetic gas tube on the top of the Gattar. Using some miscellaneous plastic parts, I mounted the wooden housing (visible in Figure 2-45) to the instrument.

Figure 2-45 *Finishing the gas tube*

9. Modify the stock

I needed a place to install the electronics, so I decided to cut into the stock. The first step was to run the stock through the band saw, cutting it in half. I'll hollow out a space in the stock for electronics, then secure the halves with screws so Wyclef can repair the guitar as needed when it's on tour.

I hollowed out a space for the electronics using Forstner bits to dig out material. Figure 2-46 shows me drilling the first hole. The guitar's power switch also needs a place to be mounted, so I cut out a hole with my dovetail saw.

Figure 2-46 *Cutting a wire hole in the electronics enclosure*

I secured the stock to the Gattar using a special attachment plate I milled. It has two sets of holes that permit Wyclef to remove a single half of the stock to make quick repairs.

Once the enclosure was ready, I soldered in the electronics. Figure 2-47 shows the inside of the stock. Putting electronics together isn't an easy task for me, but with a little trial and error, I made it work. Once the electronics were completed, I closed up the stock with screws.

Figure 2-47 *Soldering up the electronics*

10. Build the whammy trigger

One of the last-minute additions to the project is a metal trigger that will move the bridge to change the tension on the strings, therefore changing the sound. Called the vibrato or whammy, this normally takes the form of a small lever (the "whammy bar"), but in my design I decided to use the trigger to create that effect. This idea came to me when I was already working on the guitar.

I welded a couple of pieces of metal together, then used my portable band saw to cut a trigger shape.

11. Create the back panel

I created a plastic plate to cover the bridge-tensioning springs. I eventually covered it in paint to make it look like metal.

12. Paint

It was the moment of truth! I showed Wyclef the guitar and he wanted it immediately, so I spray-painted the Gattar with gold paint, unstringing it first and covering the pickups with tape. When the paint was dry, I re-strung the Gattar and it was ready to go.

Summary

The Gattar project is done, and so is this chapter. I hope you learned a bunch and found inspiration in the pages of this chapter. If you liked wood, you'll love metal! First, though, Chapter 3 explores the relatively new field of computer-controlled tools.

CNC Projects

3

I've done a lot of work with wood and metal. As you saw in Chapters 1 and 2, I build many different projects with a wide variety of tools. Two of my newest and potentially most useful tools are a pair of CNC routers, which move a rotary tool around a bed to grind out precise shapes on a piece of plastic, wood, or metal. Because they are ground-breaking tools compared to classic woodshop hardware, I'm giving CNC tools their own chapter.

First I'll describe my two CNC routers along with a mention of my favorite bits. Then I'll describe a pair of projects made with the help of CNC technology: a dart board and a sign. You can see my ShopBot Desktop in Figure 3-1.

Figure 3-1 *Cutting a shape out of plastic*

CNC Tools and Materials

Let's go over the two CNC routers I own, a ShopBot Desktop and an X-Carve, and then I'll describe some of the bits I use the most.

ShopBot Desktop

If you've heard of a CNC router, likely you've heard of ShopBot, one of the industry leaders. My ShopBot Desktop (seen in Figure 3-2) was my first CNC machine, and I have to say there was a very steep learning curve for me in getting started.

I run the ShopBot on an old HP laptop, using a pair of software packages. The first of these is Partworks 3D, a design program put out by ShopBot. The other program is VCarve Pro, which is software that manages the physical operations of the CNC router.

I like VCarve especially because it has lots of menu options. For instance, you could do a lot of vector work right in the program. When manipulating the toolpaths, VCarve lets you cut, paste, and move with ease. It also has a great preview, showing you how the cuts might look along the timeline of the job, so that if the power cuts out during a cut, I can home the toolhead again and resume the cut at the same point, re-selecting the vectors that hadn't been cut yet and creating a new cutting path.

This machine carves tiny shapes with great precision. My ice pick project (mentioned in Chapter 7) includes my logo engraved on the handles of the picks, and I use the ShopBot and a V bit to do that engraving. Part of the reason why it's so precise is that it's super heavy, minimizing wobble during carving. The machine weighs over 100 pounds thanks to its 3/8" steel frame and massive gantry. I also like how the ShopBot has an electric spindle instead of a router. This motor has a higher rate of speed than the router, keeps a consistent torque down to much lower speeds that the router can handle, and is generally quieter. I have a variable frequency drive (VFD) that controls the speed of the three-phase spindle, giving me an excellent amount of control over the toolhead.

The machine, while a really great unit, definitely caters more to professionals than hobbyists. It's expensive—$7,500 delivered—but I can rely on it to get me through pretty much any job I need to do using a CNC router. Another downside is that the ShopBot has a small footprint, able to carve on only 18" × 24" pieces of material. Despite these limitations, I use my ShopBot all the time. I had a hard time learning how to use this thing, but I'm really happy I made the jump.

Figure 3-2 *The ShopBot Desktop featuring the optional spindle (photo credit: Inventables)*

Inventables X-Carve

The X-Carve (Figure 3-3) was my second CNC machine. It comes as a kit, and this keeps the cost down for anyone wanting to get into the world of CNC carving. Your investment is about $1,000, and you are on your way. Assembling it was not easy for me, but it was simple for my high school interns to get it up and going in a few days.

X-Carve comes in a few sizes. I have the larger unit with a cutting area of about 32″ × 32″. I like the challenge of using up the entire surface of a 32″ × 32″ board to make all the parts of a design in one cut path.

I have come to like the Easel software for a few reasons, most of which is the ability to share your projects with other users. I have a few published projects, and it is nice to see others inspired to interpret my designs and make them their own.

Figure 3-3 *The X-Carve Desktop offers an easy entry into the CNC world (photo credit: Inventables)*

Router Bits

I have a bunch of bits (Figure 3-4) for my ShopBot and X-Carve, and these cut away material in different ways. Each bit has specific qualities and you need to know what you're looking for because there are literally hundreds to choose from. Nearly everything I've cut just requires vector paths, because that's just what my work requires, and this means most of my cuts are straight up and down. I'm just cutting letters, mostly, and haven't done the type of 3D models where you angle the bit to carve out a 3D shape.

I take the following criteria into consideration in selecting a bit:

Shank diameter
> I mostly use 1/4"-shank bits but 1/8" are common. However, many people swear by heavier bits, like 3/8" and 1/2", for their resistance to vibration and quieter operation.

Cutting diameter
> This governs the size of the cuts, and often, but not always, this ties into the shank diameter.

Cutting direction
> Bits come in "up-cut" and "down-cut" and this describes where the waste wood goes. Up-cut forces the chips up and out of the hole, while down-cut forces them down. A third category, compression, is a combination of the two.

The following bit styles are commonly found in a CNC workshop, but this is not an exhaustive list:

Boring bit
> Simply a short drill bit, used for making circular holes.

Plunge bit

> These bits cut smooth grooves in the material, finishing not only the sides but the bottom as well.

Ball nose bit

> These bits are used for making 3D carvings, and come in at different angles to make the shapes.

Spiral bit

> These look a lot like traditional drill bits and are used for basic cutting, and I use them all the time for creating signs.

V bit

> These arrowhead-shaped bits play many roles in a CNC project, but I use them for engraving. In my ice pick production run (described in Chapter 7), I used a V bit to etch my logo into brass stock. Most people say a 60-degree V bit is a great starting point for learning your CNC router, because it does have a lot of uses.

Surfacing

> Used to skim the surface of the material to plane it smooth.

Insert engraving system

> This product features a small carbide knife held in the bit, allowing you to make very delicate engravings.

Figure 3-4 *A variety of CNC router bits (credit: Greg Flanagan)*

Creating a Makerspace Sign

I designed and built a clock sign for a makerspace in New York called the Incubator (Inc. for short) and it consists of CNC-milled letters with old tools stuck in them with casting resin, as well as a digital clock beneath the letters.

The organization supplied the clock, which was very generic looking and boring, but also rather big. I came up with a solution where I painted the various parts to look like they were cast out of iron. You can see the final project in Figure 3-5. Follow along and I'll show you how I made it!

Figure 3-5 *The Inc. sign also helps disguise a boring-looking clock*

Tools and Materials

I used the following power tools, hand tools, and materials to build my clock:

- ShopBot Desktop CNC mill
- Table saw
- Chop saw
- LED clock
- MDF (medium-density fiberboard)
- Wood glue
- 3M Sandblaster sanding sponge
- Brad nailer
- Heat gun

- Gray spray paint
- Sophisticated Finishes iron paint
- Throwaway tools used for decoration
- EnviroTex Lite casting acrylic

Making the Sign

The sign consists of a decorative top spelling out the name of the makerspace as well as an electronic clock below it, telling visitors to the space what time it is. Here's how I built it:

1. Mill the letters and edges

I started off with a sheet of MDF in my ShopBot, carving out the letters that make up the makerspace's logo. The organization sent me a copy of its logo as an Adobe Illustrator file.

I secured the MDF to the spoilboard, the sacrificial wooden board that serves as a work surface for the machine. Then I started the ShopBot and it milled out the letters. I love MDF: it's a good clean base you can start with. It has a smooth, grainless, nondescript texture and you can paint it or change the texture. If I had used plywood, I would have had to align all the letters so the grain would match up. Since I used MDF, I could have the letters any which way with no one being the wiser. Figure 3-6 shows my ShopBot milling the letters.

Figure 3-6 *Cutting out letters on the ShopBot*

2. Clean up the letters and edges

When I designed the letters, I made sure they had tabs on them. Tabs are much thinner pieces of wood in a CNC project that haven't been milled through completely, and they're there to keep cut-out shapes from flying around. After the milling is complete, you simply cut through the tabs with a box cutter, as you see me doing in Figure 3-7. After trimming with the knife I sanded the shapes smooth using a Sandblaster sanding sponge from 3M.

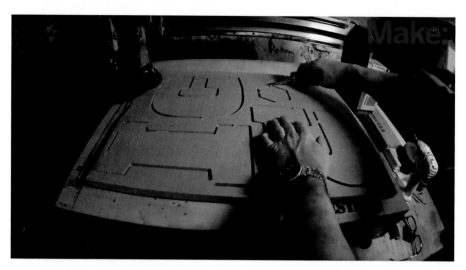

Figure 3-7 *Cutting the tabs to remove the letters*

3. Glue the edges to the letters

Each letter also has a raised bezel, an outline of the letter, and the two together resemble a shallow channel letter. Figure 3-8 shows me gluing them together with wood glue.

Figure 3-8 *Gluing the letter edges to the letters*

4. Cut boards for the box

Next I cut the various pieces of MDF for the clock enclosure as well as the decorative pieces for the front. I trimmed the MDF to the right width on my table saw and then cut down the pieces to size on my chop saw.

5. Glue the box together

I made a box shape (seen in Figure 3-9) using more pieces of MDF. First I glued each joint and then secured it with my brad nailer. This box will enclose the digital clock.

Figure 3-9 *Gluing and nailing the clock enclosure*

6. Cut the front

I cut a window into a panel of quarter-inch MDF, simply by cutting through it with my box cutter. That's how easy MDF is to work with! This panel is the bezel for the clock, as seen in Figure 3-10. I glued it into the front with clamps securing it.

Figure 3-10 *Gluing the front bezel in place*

7. Decorate the facade

The facade consists of a smaller box that will attach to the front of the clock, serving both to make it look like an iron I-beam and also to minimize the clock's profile—having a smaller shape on the front makes the whole thing look smaller. I also included a couple of decorative pieces of wood glued in, with glass beads glued onto them (Figure 3-11). These are the "rivets" in the fake I-beam.

Figure 3-11 *When painted, these glass beads will look like rivets*

8. Paint the letters

I started off with a base coat of gray spray paint, then added a second layer of Sophisticated Finishes iron metallic paint. This stuff has actual iron filings in it, which is cool and also allows you to make them rusty if you want. Sophisticated Finishes also sells an antiquing solution that is the third layer to apply. I put the solution in a spray bottle and coated the project. The solution rusts the metal dust in the paint, giving it a perfect iron finish.

9. Decorate the letters

The letters themselves have an added decoration: a background of tools like wrenches, a ruler, and a little clamp. You can see it in Figure 3-12. I had a little fun, like having the tools go through the letters, and I had a nice assortment of old tools from my junk drawer.

When I had the tools arranged just right, I mixed up and poured EnviroTex Lite casting resin into the letters; their raised edges kept it from spilling out. EnviroTex is the sort of stuff used for bar tops. It comes in a pair of bottles and is mixed 50-50. A good way to ensure you're mixing it right is simply to look at the bottles. If you start with the same amount in each bottle, when you're done the liquid levels should be the same. After I had put the EnviroTex into the letters, I worked them over with the heat gun to force the bubbles out of the resin.

Figure 3-12 *The letters are decorated with a variety of tools*

10. Attach the letters to the box

As a final step, I attached the letters to the clock enclosure with Loctite epoxy and secured them with L-brackets, as seen in Figure 3-13. The clock is done!

Figure 3-13 *Attaching the letters with epoxy and L-brackets*

Summary

This project was a great branding piece for Inc. and helped disguise a very functional clock. At the same time it helped build on my CNC skills. I love how it turned out.

Dart Board Cabinet

I am Twitter friends with the actor Eric Stonestreet, and he asked me to make him a dart board cabinet that celebrated his pet dog, Hawkins. It consists of a white oak box with the traditional double-arched doors in front, which flip open to reveal dart holders and a blackboard surface for keeping score. The front of the cabinet features a design of Hawkins (Figure 3-14) that I cut out of red oak on my ShopBot CNC mill.

Figure 3-14 *The dart board cabinet features a CNC-milled design on the front*

Tools and Materials

I used a surprisingly diverse set of tools to make the cabinet:

- Chop saw
- Table saw
- Cordless drill
- Drill press
- Plug cutter
- Palm sander
- Router
- Brad nailer
- Festool domino joiner
- Reciprocal sander
- Planer
- Oak planks
- Oak plywood
- MDF
- Clamps
- Wood glue
- Spray glue
- Stain
- Polyurethane varnish

Building the Dart Board Cabinet

I took the following steps to complete the project:

1. Cut and trim the oak planks

I ran white oak planks through my table saw, then cut them down to size on the chop saw. These boards will form the cabinet sides, top, and bottom.

2. Pre-drill the edges

I needed to attach the boards to each other very securely, so I chose to use metal screws. But I also knew the cabinet was decorative, so I wanted to make sure the screws were hidden. So I pre-drilled screw countersinks (Figure 3-15) on the ends of the side boards.

Figure 3-15 *Drilling countersinks on the ends of two of the boards*

3. Make the box

I glued and clamped the boards into a box shape, tapped the boards into place with a hammer (Figure 3-16), and then screwed them together.

Figure 3-16 *Tapping the cabinet sides square*

4. Plug the screw holes

Using a special saw called a plug cutter (seen in Figure 3-17), I cut out a bunch of pegs. Then I glued the screw holes and tapped the pegs into place, leaving a little sticking out. When the glue had dried I sawed off the extra wood with a flush cutter and sanded it smooth with a palm sander.

Figure 3-17 *Making screw-hole plugs with a plug cutter*

5. Cut a recess into the frame

I used my router to cut a groove in the edge of the box so that a piece of plywood will nest in it, forming the back of the cabinet.

6. Make the back

While the glue on the front parts was drying I made the back of the box out of a layer of oak plywood spray-glued to a layer of MDF. When it dried, I put it into the recess I cut with the router, glued it, and nailed it into place with my brad nailer.

7. Assemble the front

This consists of four planks of oak forming two doors. In the next step I'll cut a lovely curve in the front doors, but for now they're just cut at an angle. I joined each set of doors with my Festool domino jig, which cuts a slot in the edge of a board that fits a special peg called a domino tenon. You can see them in Figure 3-18. This lets me strongly and securely join boards at the edge. I clamped and glued the two doors.

Figure 3-18 *Joining two sets of boards with domino tenons*

8. Shape the front

Once the two doors had dried, I needed to give them the customary arched shape. I drew one curve freehand, then taped the two doors on top of each other and cut both at the same time on the band saw. You can see me cutting in Figure 3-19. I sanded the doors on my recipcrocating sander, ran them through the planer, then palm-sanded them smooth. I attached the doors to the cabinet with brass piano hinges.

Figure 3-19 *I drew one door's curve freehand and then cut out both boards simultaneously*

9. Cut the wood for the design

Next I switched things up and worked on my CNC. I wanted the design on the front to have kind of a rough-hewn look, so for a material I glued together strips of red oak to form a single sheet.

10. Mill the design

Before I could start milling, I needed a logo for the front. I created the design in Adobe Illustrator, and it features a dog in the center with the family name and dog's name surrounding it.

I spray-mounted the red oak to a sheet of MDF, and ran it through my ShopBot, cutting out the design. You can see the ShopBot's spindle at work in Figure 3-20. I milled down to just a millimeter or so, then used a belt sander on the reverse to sand away the tabs, allowing me to remove the letters.

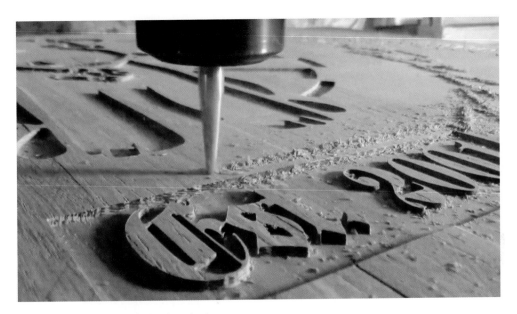

Figure 3-20 *Milling the design in red oak*

11. Add the design to the doors

After sanding them smooth, I glued the letters and design into place and tacked them down with a brad nailer. You can see me arranging things in Figure 3-21. After it dried I went in with a chisel and shaped some of the details to make them seem more rough-hewn and carved. I wanted to take the design away from a machine-cut look to more of a hand-carved look.

Figure 3-21 *Gluing the design into place*

12. Add the border

I cut out a border of red-oak strips (Figure 3-22) and glued them into place around the edge of the doors. This will help define the edge and give the cabinet a finished look.

Figure 3-22 *Adding the border of red oak strips*

13. Finish the wood

All that remained was to stain and varnish the wood. I coated it in Minwax oak stain and a couple coats of polyurethane varnish. It's done! Figure 3-23 shows the final product with the scoring chalkboards and dart racks on the inside.

Figure 3-23 *The interior of the finished dart board enclosure*

Summary

The dart board enclosure project was a great test of my CNC skills, and I love how it turned out. This chapter also has come to an end, and I hope it helped you level up your CNC milling skills.

Working with Metal

4.

I love working with metal: bending it, peening it, welding it. There's still a lot I have left to learn, and I'm always trying out new ways of shaping and cutting it. A lot of my videos came about simply because I wanted to try out a new technique.

In this chapter, I describe four metal projects I worked on recently: a steel box sign that employs a novel assembly method, a machete (seen in Figure 4-1) cut out of a saw blade, a table with aluminum legs milled on a lathe, and finally, a skull belt buckle carved out of wood and then cast in metal.

But first, I'll share a selection of my favorite metalworking tools, ranging from my trusty Delta band saw to a selection of angle grinders, as well as my all-time favorite drill press.

Figure 4-1 *In this chapter, you'll learn how I built this machete*

Tools

The following are metalworking tools I use on a daily basis. I left out more commonplace tools you might see all the time, like hammers and screwdrivers, and instead focused on the big-ticket machines I use in my videos.

Beaumont Belt Sander

Sometimes people ask why I'm using a belt sander to sand metal. I reply that the Beaumont is a belt sander made to sand metal—it's really for knife making—but I use it for everything. It's got a 2" × 72" belt and a 2 HP, 3-speed motor. You can change the grits, and you can change the speed by jumping the pulleys, making this a versatile tool in my shop. I use it pretty much every day.

I actually have two Beaumonts. One I've owned for about a year and a half (you can see it in Figure 4-2), and it's starting to get a little beat up. I bought it from the manufacturer in Ohio, a small company that makes each sander to order. I got another one recently. One of my fans was moving and couldn't take it with him, and asked if I wanted to buy it. Now I'll have one for my shop on the Lower East Side and one for my place in the Catskills.

Figure 4-2 *The Beaumont belt sander was made as a tool for knife makers*

Bridgeport Vertical Mill

Think of the Bridgeport as sort of a big drill press (seen in Figure 4-3) but with a powered X and Y bed, allowing you to precisely mill steel.

According to the serial number, my Bridgeport's from 1965. A friend of a friend of a friend was moving his shop and basically gave it away. It cost a lot of money to get it to my house in the Catskills from Jersey City. It came with a vise, indexing head, and a bunch of tooling.

I just replaced the motor. The new one is three-phase, and I have a variable-frequency drive (VFD) to control it. This system gives me a finer control over the mill motor's speed.

Figure 4-3 *The Bridgeport vertical mill precisely carves material out of a block of metal*

Chopping Band Saw

I have three chopping band saws. These tools offer the ability to cleanly cut out thick sections of metal—say, a 4" block of brass or steel. Tilt the bed, and it can cut metal at angles.

My main chopping band saw was a gift from Craftsman when I did a TV show called *Hammered*. It's not the highest quality, but it works great for me, and the same blade has been on it six years. It features a 72" long by 3/4" wide blade with 6 TPI (tooth per inch), which is pretty aggressive for a metal-cutting band saw.

I also have a Kalamazoo chopping band saw I rescued from the New York City seaport where it was about to get scrapped for metal. I leave it outside because it doesn't fit in my shop, and mice make nests inside of it. I just put a tarp on it when I'm not cutting on it.

Delta Band Saw

This is my go-to band saw. A lot of time I use it with wood, but if I slow it down with pulley reduction, I can cut metal with it. If you're going to get the first tool for your workshop, I always tell people to get a band saw. You can cut straights if you put a deep blade on it, you can cut curves, and you can cut metal, wood, plastic, and leather. It's definitely a great tool to have if you're just getting started.

I like the classic 14" Delta because it has easily adjustable guides—a lot of band saws require keys to adjust the lower guides, but the Delta has knobs so you can do it by hand. The Delta has the same design from the '30s through the '90s. They have the same cast-iron arm—they're sturdy machines. The controls are all the same, and have always been the same throughout that time period.

I own three Deltas. One I purchased in a whole-shop buyout in 1990, and I paid about $100 for it. I also have one I've had since I was five or six years old; my dad got it and now it's mine. This design is slowly going out of style after all these years, but I like this kind of band saw the best.

Butterfly Die Filer

My die filer is my latest acquisition. It's like a jigsaw, but it has a file instead of a saw blade. It's probably from the 1940s. I bought it for $100 from a machine shop that was closing. The machine came with two boxes of files for it; they just swap in and out with a set screw. It was a great acquisition and I'm glad I picked it up.

Die Grinder

I use a variety of die grinders in my workshop. One of my favorites is the pneumatic angle die grinder seen in Figure 4-4. It uses quick-screw-on Scotch-Brite pads that swap in and out in seconds. I also have an inline grinder, which is basically the same except not angled. I also have a DeWalt electric die grinder, which is a heavier and more unwieldy tool but doesn't need a compressor.

All three of these grinders have a quarter-inch shank, making my tools interchangeable between the three. I also have a smaller, "mini die grinder" with a 1/8" shank, similar to Dremel tools, and it just plugs into the air hose. It's great for small projects.

Figure 4-4 *Using a die grinder to clean up a project*

Walker Turner Drill Press

I love this type of drill press. I use it for both metal and wood, changing the bit and jumping the pulleys depending on the material.

The particular model shown in Figure 4-5 has been in my family for a long time. My dad bought it at least 30 years ago—I guess I was about 17 or 18. It's a bench top for the shorter pole—the other two Walker-Turners I own are floor models.

I have my second Walker Turner set up with a mortising jig. I bought it off a violin maker here on the Lower East Side about seven years ago—I think I paid $50. The other one I keep up in my place in upstate New York.

Figure 4-5 *The Walker Turner drill press*

Gas Forge

I have a gas forge, essentially an electric-start propane burner with an insulated firebox, rapidly heating up whatever goes in there. I got it from a farrier supply store, and it's meant for people making their own horseshoes.

Grizzly Industrial Drill Press

The Grizzly drill press (Figure 4-6) is sort of a baby milling machine, like the Bridgeport but (relatively) smaller and lighter. This machine I can at least lug through my basement door.

I got the Grizzly for free. A shop was closing, and I happened to be there at the right place at the right time. It's about an $800 machine, but it's not the highest of quality. It's gotten me through some projects, so I have a greater appreciation for it now than when I first got it.

Figure 4-6 *The Grizzly drill press has a powered X and Y bed*

Plasma Cutter

This handy tool, seen in Figure 4-7, cuts conductive metals with the help of a plasma arc. It's a great way to cut metal in situations where a saw would be too slow or unwieldy.

Figure 4-7 *The plasma cutter burns through steel in seconds*

DeWalt Portable Band Saw

I use this handheld band saw (Figure 4-13) more as a benchtop cutoff tool. I keep it in a vise, and I can swing by and make quick cuts as needed. It doesn't have a trigger lock, so for bigger jobs I just put a clamp on it.

Figure 4-8 *The DeWalt portable band saw, clamped to my workbench*

Propane Torch

I always keep a few of these torches around. They consist of a small propane tank with an electrical ignition on the burner. If I have two hands free, I like to use two torches for twice as much heat that much faster.

I have the automatic pull trigger on my torches, so whenever I leave the shop I secure the trigger so if it falls down it doesn't accidentally turn on, and I also make the habit of laying them on their side when not in use.

Riveter and Pop Rivets

I use rivets in situations where I wouldn't want to use a screw. They fit into a little gun (seen in Figure 4-9) and when the handles on the gun are squeezed, the rivet is set.

Figure 4-9 *Riveting a piece of sheet metal*

Sandblasting Box

This tool uses blown sand to clean off small objects, like rust from a piece of iron. The holes in front have protective gloves built into them so you can operate the gun safely. I got mine from Tractor Supply, and I think I paid $70–75 for it.

DeWalt Metal Shears

These shears literally cut sheet metal like it was paper. The shears (seen in Figure 4-10) consist of three blades, and actually make two simultaneous cuts, removing a tiny strip of metal. Because of the way its blades are set up, the shears leave a perfectly flat cut on either side of the line. Sometimes when you use scissors on something, you end up marring both sides of the cut. This one gives you a nice clean cut.

Figure 4-10 *My DeWalt metal shears cut metal like paper*

South Bend Lathe

I have two South Bend lathes, a 9" and a 16". The smaller one is from the 1950s. I bought it in Chinatown. It was in the window of an old machine shop. Everything in the block seemed to be closing and being turned into condos, so I walked into the shop and asked if it was for sale. He said he had to think about it. The owner called me back a couple of hours later and sold it to me for $500. I've had it in my shop in the Lower East Side. It's served me well for eight years.

The bigger lathe (seen in Figure 4-11) is new to me but built in 1944. I bought it over the summer and have it up in my place in upstate New York. This lathe does it all, and I turn both wood and metal on it. I bought it from a man who was very meticulous, thankfully, and he kept it in really good shape. Now it's up to me to maintain it. It cost me $2,300 and I moved it myself from around 160 miles away on a trailer.

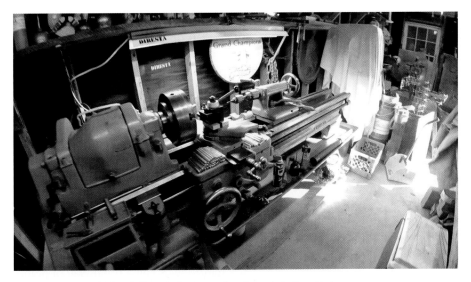

Figure 4-11 *My 16" South Bend lathe in my shop in upstate New York*

Vulcan Anvil

I'm not into blacksmithing per se, but I do use a variety of anvils for all the reasons you ordinarily would: pounding and shaping metal. I bought my Vulcan anvil off Craigslist before the big blacksmithing boom. It was $100 about 10 years ago. By contrast, I recently got a smaller Vulcan from an antique shop for $100, and it needed a new work surface.

Welders

I use a bunch of welders in my shop, but my go-to machines include a Lincoln Electric precision 225 TIG welder, as well as another pair of machines from Lincoln: a MP210 multipurpose welder that can make TIG, MIG, and stick welds, and a Square Wave TIG 200.

Wilton Bullet Vise

This vise looks great, but that's because I restored it. I found it at the recycling plant, and it was destined to be thrown into a dumpster and shipped off to Hong Kong for recycling. I cleaned it up and it has been a fixture on my workbench.

Band Saw–Cut Steel Sign

Some time ago, I received a call from Brompton, a company that makes folding bikes. They wanted a light-up steel sign with their logo for their store's cafe. We designed a box sign (Figure 4-12) that would hang from the ceiling, with a light inside to make it light up. The cafe has sort of a brushed metal look, and I made the sign to match. I cut the letters and logo out of stainless steel, and assembled the rest of the sheet of metal into the sides and back.

Part of the reason I love this project was the challenge of using a band saw to cut letters out of a four-foot sign. Because the neck of the saw rises, it prevented me from rotating a large sheet, so I had to cut it down to a smaller size to work with. Once the parts were cut out, I reassembled the sheets back into a single plate, without anyone knowing the difference.

The reason I used this technique is that the customer wanted the sign quickly. Ordinarily I'd send it out to be CNC'd by a service, but what if they messed it up? I wouldn't be able to turn it around in time. Instead, I decided to take this route, which was a lot more work, but I knew it would be delivered as promised. This also gave me the chance to try out a new technique. I love the idea of cutting apart and reattaching a sheet of metal and have no one know.

In addition to the low-tech construction technique, I also got old-school with the back-lighting, opting for classic fluorescent tubes rather than the LED strips everyone uses now. This sign might have been my last one ever with tubes. Maybe this is the day of CNC-cut signs and LED light strips, but cutting a sign out of a band saw is still a great way of doing it, and the sign ended up fitting in perfectly with the cafe's decor.

I'm going to show you how to build your own. First, however, let's explore the tools and supplies you'll need.

Figure 4-12 *This metal box sign took a new metalworking technique to complete*

Tools and Materials

You'll need the following tools to build the sign. You should recognize all of the bigger tools from the beginning of this chapter:

- DeWalt power shears
- Delta band saw
- MIG and TIG welders
- Pneumatic die grinder
- 4-1/2" angle grinder with 50-grit sanding disk
- Circular saw with a metal-cutting blade
- Riveter and pop rivets
- 1/4" hand file

You'll also need assorted materials:

- 14-gauge steel sheet
- Spray adhesive
- Cutting fluid
- Angle iron
- Presto Black Gel (*http://sculpt.com*)
- Permalac lacquer
- Frosted 1/8" acrylic
- Lexel silicone caulk adhesive
- Eyelets
- Fluorescent light fixtures
- Clamp connector

Making the Sign

The central technique of this project consists of cutting apart and then welding together a sheet of steel so that no one can tell the difference. The main reason I used this technique is that the band saw has only a small work area—too small for a 44" sign. In order to cut out the letters and other details—even the small part at the top that says Cafe—I needed to cut it into pieces on the band saw so I could move the metal around properly.

Let's go over what it takes:

1. Cut the material to size

I quickly cut a piece of 14-gauge steel down to the right size, using metal power shears and cutting fluid. It wasn't super critical to get the edge perfect, because I knew I'd be smoothing down the edges later on when I added the sides.

2. Apply the pattern

I found the center line of the front plate and drew a line to guide placing the pattern. Then I applied spray adhesive onto the metal and laid down the printout. I folded the paper in half to ensure that I centered it properly.

3. Start cutting!

I cut directly into the pattern with my band saw, using a 1/8" blade and cutting fluid. The blade starts getting dull fairly quickly, and its "side capacity," or its ability to make turns, started to go.

I eventually resorted to pre-drilling holes at locations on the letters where I was going to have to turn the material. Having a hole there gives the blade room to move around.

Because of this, I used the saw blade as more of a shaping instrument, cutting away the steel in small parts. You don't have to run the blade around the edge of the letter and have a perfect A or F fall out! I took the shortest amount of distance to get from one letter to the other, cutting across the space between the letters, as shown in Figure 4-13. I knew I'd have to go back in and fix those cuts.

Figure 4-13 *Cutting out letters*

Finally, I didn't worry about keeping the letters perfect. For one thing I knew I'd have to smooth them down with a file no matter what. That said, smooth cuts will reduce the amount of elbow grease you'll need later. Also, when people look at the sign they look at the entirety of it, and no one's measuring them with a micrometer to ensure perfection. Visually, if it looks right, I feel it *is* right.

4. Fill in the cuts

I started off using a MIG welder, but switched to a TIG welder. I found it was a little less sparky and more controlled, giving me the ability to seal up the tiny cuts in the letters, as seen in Figure 4-14. I made sure not to focus too much on one area of the design, as sheet metal warps if it gets too hot.

Figure 4-14 *Welding up the cuts after I've finished with the letters*

5. Remove the design

Once I'm done with my main cuts, I'm free to remove the paper and adhesive with some acetone. That said, I always try to keep the graphic lines on the material as long as possible.

6. Clean up the metal

The sign's steel has to look good. What's the point of using this technique if my sign looks like Frankenstein's monster? I began by filling in the cuts where I had to run the saw blade though the piece to get at a letter.

Next I used a grinder to polish down the letters with a 50-grit disk, then grabbed a die grinder (seen in Figure 4-15) to flatten out as many burrs as I could reach. While I was grinding and polishing, I kept an eye out for creases in the metal from the cuts, and went in and filled them in with the welder as needed. After that I worked on the metal with hand files, smoothing down the parts the die grinder couldn't reach.

Figure 4-15 *Grinding and filing the metal to get it looking great*

7. Reattach the side plates

Once I was ready to reassemble the front of the sign, I laid the plates out the way I wanted them and secured them with a few tack welds before going in and filling in all the gaps. I moved from part to part to ensure that the metal didn't overheat.

I had to reinforce the reassembled plates by welding the joints from the back as well. I found that I had ground off so much material on the front that I'd weakened the welds, so I strengthened them from behind.

8. Build the frame

The 14-gauge sheet metal of the signs has a tendency to flex, so I knew I'd need some angle iron (Figure 4-16) for a frame. I cut the angle iron to match the dimensions of the final sign and welded it together with my MIG. Once the frame was done, I welded it onto the face of the sign. I also included a couple of horizontal bars across the center of the sign's face, because I knew it'd need additional reinforcement.

Figure 4-16 *Welding angle iron to the edges*

9. Build the sides

Once the front panel was done, it was time to work on the sides. I cut four identical strips of the material, using a piece of angle iron to guide my circular saw.

Once they're cut to size, I clamped the side plates to the frame and welded them into place. I overlapped the front of the sign over the sides by about an eighth of an inch, allowing me to make the edges straight. I simply ground off that excess material to make a perfect corner.

10. Weld on the back frame

I reinforced the back of the box (Figure 4-17) by welding on more angle iron. The basic metal structure of the sign is nearly complete! All that it needs is the back plate installed.

Figure 4-17 *Welding on the back frame*

11. Tone and protect

Steel is great, but it has a tendency to discolor and rust. I used a blackener called Presto gel. I painted the Presto over the surface with a paintbrush, then rubbed it in with Scotch-Brite pads and #000 steel wool.

I topped it off with a couple coats of Permalac clear lacquer to protect the steel against corrosion. You can see the sign's progress in Figure 4-18.

Figure 4-18 *Spraying down the sign with clear lacquer to protect against rust*

12. Add the acrylic

The sign's letters and logos are backed by frosted acrylic. I recycled some old material from a past project. At $200 a sheet, acrylic can be pretty expensive! I cut out the shapes on the table saw and glued them into place on the inside of the sign's face.

I used Lexel, a heavy-duty silicone that has a crazy fume to it. Lexel is made to stick dissimilar surfaces together, making it perfect for this application.

13. Attach the eyelets

I drilled two holes in the top of the sign, making sure I cut through small lengths of angle iron I'd welded onto the frame. Then I inserted a pair of heavy-duty eye bolts and secured them with washers and nuts.

14. Install the lights

I'm from an old-school sign making background and I didn't immediately think of using LEDs. The sign ended up six inches deep, and if I'd gone with an LED strip I probably wouldn't have needed to have it quite that deep. On the other hand, it does give the sign a lot of presence as well. I placed the light fixtures (seen in Figure 4-19) on the back plate, and drilled the holes to mount them. Working from the underside of the plate, I pop-riveted the fixtures into place. The power cord for the lights comes out of the back of the sign.

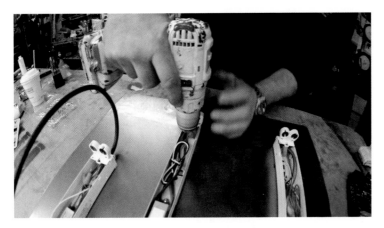

Figure 4-19 *Drilling rivet holes in the back of the sign*

15. Secure the back

Once the sign was ready to close up, I screwed the back panel in place with self-tapping screws drilled directly into the angle iron.

16. Glue on the details

I used more Lexel silicone to secure the insides of the A's and O's, as well as the "Brompton" part of the sign in the middle. The Lexel takes a while to set, so I left the pieces taped until I installed the sign the next day.

17. Install the sign

I was pleasantly surprised that the dark, brownish metal details of the cafe matched those of the sign. I installed a mounting bracket made out of 1" pieces of steel bolted directly into the cafe's exposed I-beams and plugged it into a handy outlet. Figure 4-20 shows us installing the sign.

Figure 4-20 *David and I install the finished sign in Brompton's cafe*

Summary

This sign was a great challenge for my band saw skills, and extremely satisfying to build because it came together so perfectly, while showing off some classic signmaking techniques.

Vampire Table

I came up with the idea for this project when I found a cool piece of wood in the garbage. It had big old 8" nails stuck into it and I thought, wouldn't it be cool if they were the legs of a table? Now, six or seven years later, it's finally coming to fruition—though not necessarily how I first pictured it.

The table consists of a 4" cross-section of maple I bought a few years ago at a sawmill in upstate New York, with a trio of 2"-thick aluminum spikes apparently pounded through the disc, and they serve as the table's legs. Figure 4-21 shows the finished build. I call it the Vampire Table because the spikes remind me of the silver stakes used to kill cinematic vampires.

Figure 4-21 *I built this table to look like the spikes had been pounded through the wood*

Tools and Materials

I used the following tools and materials in this project:

- Kalamazoo chopping band saw
- South Bend 16" lathe with a chamfer for securing the material
- Palm sander

- Aluminum rod, with three lengths cut from a 5′ length of 2″ stock
- Big piece of wood
- Polyurethane varnish

Building the Table

I followed these steps to build my table:

1. Cut the aluminum rods

I used my Kalamazoo chopping band saw (seen in Figure 4-22) to cut three 19″ lengths of 2″-thick, 6262-T6511 aluminum purchased from onlinemetals.com.

Figure 4-22 *Cutting the aluminum rod with a chopping band saw*

2. Mill the spikes

I attached the first rod to my South Bend lathe. I began to mill it using a tapering jig to create the sharp-looking appearance of the legs. The South Bend is a great tool with different speed and torque settings depending on what you want to do. In the early stages of milling the spikes I made deep passes with a rough bit, which dug out a lot of material, and I used a back gear on the lathe with a slow speed and a lot of strength. It really helps carve out a lot of material.

When I had the general shape right, I sped up the lathe and made a finishing pass with a finer bit. You can see me partway through the pass in Figure 4-23.

Figure 4-23 *The finishing pass smooths down the aluminum considerably*

3. Polish the spikes

While the spikes were still spinning on the lathe, I worked them over with a palm sander with a couple of different grits, culminating in a very fine 320 grit to help bring out the polish. I used the palm sander while the spike was spinning to eliminate any lines left over from milling.

Then I ran steel wool over the spikes, polishing them up by increasing the fineness of the wool, starting out fairly rough and then working up to #000.

4. Prepare the tabletop

I found a great piece of maple at a sawmill in upstate New York. I think it was $20 and it had been sitting around my house for the past few years. It's about four inches thick, end grain, with a giant split cutting into it.

I belt-sanded the piece of maple, then worked on it with the disc sander. There were a lot of deep chain saw marks left by the guy who'd cut it down, and the fact that it was end grain didn't help either. Figure 4-24 shows me working on the piece of maple with the disc sander.

Figure 4-24 *Sanding the piece of maple*

5. Mark the drill holes

I wanted the three spikes to be equidistant, so I used a compass to measure the distances between them. I marked the wood with drill holes using a permanent marker.

6. Drill the holes

I tried a couple ways of drilling the 2" holes that the spike legs will go through. At first I tried a battery-powered drill using a Forstner bit, but switched to a corded drill for the extra power. However, the main problem was that the bit had a tendency to "walk." This happens when the bit isn't drilling into the wood, and instead moves around randomly, making a mess of the wood.

My solution was to start the hole in a two-by-four clamped to the log section, as seen in Figure 4-25. It still walked a little but wasn't as bad. The angles were random. I didn't want the legs to look too orderly; I wanted them to look like they had been flung through the wood, not placed there precisely.

Having drilled a hole, I made a test fit with a spike. I wanted the holes to be slightly smaller than the spikes, ensuring the aluminum had a nice tight fit. After that I drilled the other two holes.

Figure 4-25 *Using a two-by-four jig to ensure the Forstner bit didn't "walk"*

7. Finish the spikes

Having got the tabletop to a good stopping point, I worked on the spikes again. I wanted them to look like they were hammered through the surface. I banged on the ends with a hammer to make them look more like nails and to give the ends a little character.

Next, I polished them up on the buffing wheel and brought out as much polish as possible. Having worked my way back from sandpaper to steel wool and finally to the buffing wheel, I had the spikes really looking great.

8. Finish the tabletop

Next, I worked on finishing the table portion. I began by sanding the holes some with the disk sander because the bit's walking had marred the wood.

Then I worked on polishing the wood. I began with linseed oil but over the course of four or five days I probably poured the entire can of oil into the surface. It just soaked right in, and nothing stayed at the surface. Over the next few days I gave it a few coats of satin polyurethane as well.

When I'd built up enough coats of polyurethane, I palm-sanded it very smooth and gave it a wax finish. You can see how the table looks in Figure 4-26.

Figure 4-26 *The finished tabletop, sanded and waxed*

9. Add the spikes

As a final step I inserted the spikes and pounded them into place (Figure 4-27) with a rubber mallet. I periodically measured the length of the legs sticking out to ensure the top of the table remained level.

Figure 4-27 *Tapping in the legs with a rubber mallet*

One thing people ask about is the split in the wood. Everyone's expecting a bow tie, which keeps this kind of split from getting bigger. I decided against it; it's a little too cliched and expected. Anyway, the table is for my own use, and not going to a customer's house, so if the table breaks, I'll just fix it!

The finished table looks appropriately epic with its gleaming wood and polished metal.

Summary

The Vampire Table has a beautiful wooden top, but it's the aluminum spikes I milled on the lathe that really give it character. The legs look like they were thrown through the top by Zeus, and that's what I wanted. It was a fun project and rare for me in that it's a piece of furniture going into my home.

Cutting a Machete out of a Saw

I wanted to make a machete out of a section of metal saw. I'd bought a crosscut saw from an antique store in Philadelphia for 20 bucks. I cut the machete shape out of the blade using a plasma cutter, then finished the blade on the grinder and sander. I attached the blade to a handle I made out of ziricote wood and bronze. You can see the finished machete in Figure 4-28. Read on to learn how I made it.

Figure 4-28 *I made this machete out of a saw blade*

Tools and Materials

These are the parts and materials I used in making my machete:

- An old saw
- FastCap pattern-marker
- Band saw
- Plasma cutter

- Drill press
- Step bits
- Ziricote wood
- 1/8" bronze plate
- Brass stock
- Palm sander
- Bristle disk
- Bastard file
- Rattail file
- Scotch-Brite
- Steel wool
- Buffing wheel

Making the Machete

I followed these steps to assemble and finish the machete:

1. Draw the design

I drew the machete shape I wanted to use with a permanent marker on a piece of particle board, seen in Figure 4-29. I more or less drew it by hand, thinking of the shape of a similar machete that I own. I made a template to help me cut out a machete from the saw blade.

Figure 4-29 *Drawing the design on a piece of scrap wood*

2. Cut out the template

The next step was to cut out the inside of the template. I ran it through the band saw and cut out the inside, creating a guide for the torch of my plasma cutter.

I laid the template on the saw blade and clamped it into place. A lot of people ask me why I didn't use the back of the saw as the back of the machete blade. That was because I knew I'd still be able to use the saw afterwards.

3. Cut out the machete

I cut out the shape with the plasma cutter (Figure 4-30), tracing the inside of the wooden template. I didn't polish up the metal first because I wanted to preserve that corroded texture, though the saw was so rusty the plasma cutter didn't want to complete a circuit. It took a little longer than I expected, but I finished cutting and popped out the blade.

Figure 4-30 *Burning through steel with a plasma cutter*

4. Clean up the metal

I cleaned up the blade on the belt sander, smoothing down the rough edges left by the plasma cutter. I also sanded a couple of millimeters past the part where the steel lost its temper. I didn't re-temper it, but it's not like I'm going to hack through a jungle with it, either.

I caved in and decided to polish up the flat of the blade rather than leaving it rusty. I smoothed it down with the belt sander, then cleaned up the blade with a palm sander (Figure 4-31) with a bristle disc from 3M.

Figure 4-31 *The palm sander helps remove corrosion*

5. Begin shaping the bevel

While I was sanding, I started working the bevel, seen in Figure 4-32. This is where the metal thins out to form the edge. Of course I didn't fully sharpen the blade at this point, to save on cuts and nicks.

Figure 4-32 *Shaping the bevel to bring the metal to an edge*

6. Drill the peg holes

Next, I cut the holes in the handle that I'll use to attach the wood to the metal. I had a really hard time drilling the spring steel, since I didn't have the right kind of bit in-house. I eventually resorted to step drill bits, and that did the trick.

7. Mill the pegs

Then I made the brass pegs that will keep the handle on. I put a piece of brass stock on the lathe and milled it down to fit the holes in the handle. I didn't worry about getting the width perfect, because I knew they would be peened over.

8. Cut out the handles

Then I traced the handle (Figure 4-33) on a piece of ziricote wood from Belize. I changed the design a little from the metal, adding a finger tab that will keep the fingers from slipping onto the blade. I made it a little bigger than I wanted, knowing that I'd be sanding and filing it down.

I cut out the handle on the band saw, then traced the handle onto another piece of ziricote using a marker, and then cut that one out too. Together these pieces of wood will form the handle.

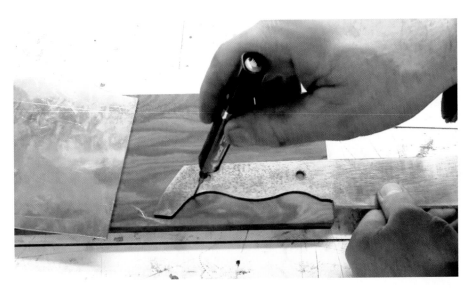

Figure 4-33 *Tracing the handles on ziricote wood*

9. Add the bronze

Once I had the handles cut out, I traced them onto some 1/8" bronze plate. I'm going to sandwich the knife blade between two layers of bronze, as well as the ziricote.

I drilled the holes in the bronze (Figure 4-34), tapping the hole locations in order to give the drill something to grab onto. The bronze drilled much easier than the saw blade's spring steel! Then I used the finished plate as a template to drill the other.

Figure 4-34 *Drilling the bronze plates*

10. Shape the handle

I began the process of finishing the handle. The goal was to make the handle more comfortable to hold. First, however, I needed to put the handle together temporarily. I used that first bronze plate to drill the peg holes in the wooden handles.

Then I tapped wooden sticks into the peg holes to temporarily stack them together for sanding. I wanted to smooth down and level the part by the blade, which I couldn't do with the blade in it.

Then I took it back apart, added the blade, and put the sticks back in to secure it. I still used the wooden sticks because I didn't want to sand those brass pegs until I knew how long they'd need to be. I brought it to the sander (Figure 4-35) and began working on it.

Figure 4-35 *Shaping the handle on the belt sander*

After sanding it for a while, I realized I had too much material remaining, and brought the handle back to the band saw. Eventually, after going back and forth between the sander and the saw, I got the handle looking the way I wanted it.

11. Assemble the machete

I cut the brass pegs down from the rod I'd milled on the lathe, then mixed up some West System epoxy and glued the handle in place with the pegs keeping everything together.

When the glue had dried, I smoothed down everything on the belt sander, as seen in Figure 4-36.

Figure 4-36 *Sanding the glued handle*

12. Finish the machete

I kept at it with the sander, as well as files, just trying to get that real organic shape that would make the handle comfortable to grip. I worked at it with bastard and rattail files, as well as a strip of an old sanding belt. When I was done sanding, I went to work with Scotch-Brite pads, steel wool, and my buffing wheel to bring out the shine in the wood.

I coated the handle in Briwax to give it a little more polish and protection from dirt. The final step is sharpening the blade with 200- or 300-grit sandpaper.

Summary

I love making my own tools and this machete was no different. I had an idea for a machete and it worked out exactly as I intended.

Skull-and-Crossbones Belt Buckle

I created a skull-and-crossbones belt buckle almost by accident. I had just gotten a GoPro camera and mounted it to a piece of padauk wood, and set it to record—I was mostly playing around to test it, and started sketching a skull motif.

Pretty soon I decided I was going to make a belt buckle. I carved it out of wood, then made a mold of that wooden positive and poured in casting metal to make a metal duplicate. Figure 4-37 shows how it turned out.

Follow along and I'll show you how I made it.

Figure 4-37 *I'll show you how I made this sweet belt buckle*

Tools and Supplies

I used these parts and materials to make my buckle:

- Marker
- Wood-carving tools
- Padauk wood
- Band saw
- Polyurethane
- Baby powder
- Torch
- Crucible
- White casting metal, bought from Contenti Jewelry Supply (*https://contenti.com/*)
- Steel rod

Make the Buckle

I followed these steps to create my belt buckle:

1. Sketch the design

I drew the design on padauk wood using a permanent marker. You can see me working on the skull-and-crossbones design in Figure 4-38.

Figure 4-38 *Sketching the design on a piece of padauk wood*

2. Carve it out

I carved around the edge of the shape with a chisel, defining the main motif of the skull. I try to bring the background down and leave the object forward. Even the crossbones go down a layer, though they're higher up than the background.

I go back and forth with a chisel and a file. I like to sand and carve until the final shape takes form. Once the drawn design gets carved away, I'm literally freestyling, trying to find what I want in the wood. You can see the carving's progress in Figure 4-39.

Figure 4-39 *The carving continues*

3. Cut out the carving

Once I had the carving the way I wanted it, I cut it out on my band saw. I was careful to angle the wood so it cut it out in a taper—the back is wider than the front. This makes it easier to pull it out of the mold. Having cut it out, I cleaned up the edge to define it a little better.

As a final step, I coated the wooden shape in polyurethane, then allowed it to dry. Figure 4-40 shows the buckle ready for casting!

Figure 4-40 *Coating the form in polyurethane*

4. Make the mold

My mold is just some pieces of wood bolted together. I dusted the buckle in baby powder to help its removal, then put it into the frame, face up.

I packed the frame with delft clay, applying it by hand as shown in Figure 4-41 and then pounding it really tight with a rubber mallet.

Finally, I added a pair of screws in the back to help remove the wooden form. I have my mold!

Figure 4-41 *Adding delft clay to the mold*

5. Bend the buckle's chape

The *chape* is the part that attaches the buckle to the belt. I used a torch and bent up a piece of 1/8" steel rod. Figure 4-42 shows the chape in progress. I will put it in with the molten metal to attach it to the front plate of the buckle.

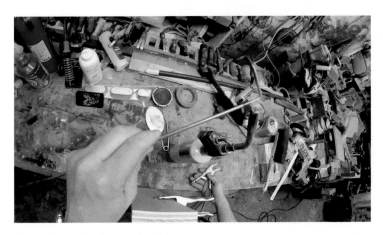

Figure 4-42 *Bending up the chape*

6. Pour the metal

I'm using a generically named product called white casting metal. It melts at around 400 degrees, making it easy to soften using a crucible and propane torch. When I had the metal good and hot, I poured a bunch of it from my crucible into the mold.

While the metal was still molten, I dropped in the chape and poured a little more casting metal on top of it, melting directly from the ingot of casting metal. Figure 4-43 shows the buckle with the chape securely attached to the back.

Figure 4-43 *Casting the buckle with the chape embedded*

7. Finish the buckle

After it had cooled, I pulled the buckle out of the mold, sprayed it with black spray paint, and then rubbed it with steel wool (Figure 4-44) to give it a darker and more aged look.

Figure 4-44 *The finished buckle. It just needs a belt!*

Summary

This chapter went all-out with tons of information, beginning with what tools I reach for first in my metalworking projects, then exploring four very different metal-based projects I've worked on recently. In Chapter 5 I share some projects I make with plastic, a very flexible, capable material.

Plastic Projects

Having worked as toymaker, I have a lot of experience using plastic in my projects. In a way, plastic is an overly broad category because bending styrene (as seen in Figure 5-1) offers a vastly different experience from casting resin or heat-bending acrylic. In this chapter, I'll share some tips on working with styrene, a commonplace plastic sold in sheet form and used in a variety of ways. After that I'll share two of my plastic-related projects: a chess set cast using Smooth-On, a low-viscosity casting resin, as well as a light-up sign with styrene channel letters.

Figure 5-1 *I love using Styrene in my projects*

Working with Styrene

Chances are, you already use styrene on a daily basis. For instance, those white plastic lids for coffee cups? Styrene. It comes in a variety of thicknesses up to 1/4" and responds to cutting, bending, heating, and painting.

In lieu of covering a selection of plastic-working tools (which mostly have already been described), I'm going to describe some of my favorite techniques when working with styrene.

Bending

Thin enough styrene can be bent without heating. You can see me shaping a strip of styrene in Figure 5-2, bending it around a screwdriver held in a vise. The material does have a degree of tension to it, and when you try to get it to bend, you may need to clamp it into place while waiting for the glue to cure.

Figure 5-2 *Shaping styrene with a screwdriver held in a vise*

Cutting

Styrene works really easily: you slice it and snap it. For the thinner stuff I find a ruler and box cutter do the trick. You can also cut it with ordinary saws, though it is a messy job with a lot of burrs left on the cut. Figure 5-3 shows me cutting into styrene with a Dremel.

Figure 5-3 *You can easily cut styrene with a Dremel*

Heating

Another way to work with styrene involves heating it. This makes the styrene into a wet noodle, essentially, and most of the time it's difficult to work with in this state. Mostly I let gravity do the work. In Figure 5-4 you can see me heating up styrene with a blowtorch to help the material hug the form underneath.

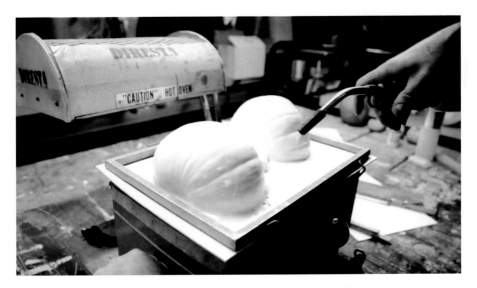

Figure 5-4 *Heating styrene makes it very flexible—sometimes too much so*

Joining

You can attach pieces of styrene together easily. I mostly use Weld-On methylene chloride. It's a solvent that works as a glue by melting two surfaces and sticking them together.

I find the best way to handle solvent is a small squeeze bottle with needle applicator. It puts the solvent precisely where I want it (Figure 5-5), and if the needle gets clogged I can always loosen it up with a cigarette lighter.

Finally, you can get really clean joints by letting them overlap. Just cut off the excess and sand them smooth after the solvent cures.

Figure 5-5 *Gluing two pieces of styrene together with solvent*

Patching

Filling holes in styrene can be problematic, because most fillers won't stick to the material at all. I sometimes use acetone to soften plastic wood. When I've thinned the plastic wood sufficiently, I goop it on (Figure 5-6) and let it cure. Much like the Weld-On, acetone is a solvent that etches into the plastic and helps the plastic wood stick.

Figure 5-6 *I seal up cracks in my styrene projects with plastic wood thinned with acetone*

Smoothing

Styrene responds to filing and sanding, either with sandpaper or hand files. In the latter case I suggest a half-round file, though I also use flat files, as seen in Figure 5-7. If I sand away too much material, I slather on some jet acrylic. This is the stuff dentists use to make temporary crowns, and it can be used to bulk up the styrene to build up thin spots.

Figure 5-7 *Filing down the edges of a styrene box*

Vacuforming

One of styrene's best uses is as a medium for a vacuum former, seen in Figure 5-8. The vacuform simultaneously heats the styrene while sucking down on it with a vacuum, causing it to coat a form. My vacuformer comfortably works up to three inches, so if I want to create bigger shapes, I need to create two or more panels, and then glue them together.

Figure 5-8 *Softening and shaping a piece of styrene in a vacuum former*

You can either vacuform with positive form or a negative form. With a positive shape you're looking to coat the outside of object with the plastic.

One disadvantage of this technique is that the styrene coats the shape and softens the detail, because the surface that touches the form is on the inside. If you do vacuform over a positive, make sure the styrene gets very hot so it will coat every cranny of the shape. There's always an annoying curve where the styrene rises tentlike to cover the form. When I think I might encounter this, I make a point to place the form on a quarter-inch piece of wood so I can cut off that curvy shape.

If you're vacuforming a very detailed shape, I definitely suggest making a negative form out of plaster, like the one seen in Figure 5-9. The outside of the plastic coats the form, making the crispest possible impression of the original.

Figure 5-9 *Vacuforming styrene with a negative form*

Casting a Chess Set

I wanted to make the classic chess set (Figure 5-10) of dime-store lore. Think of the hollow black and white plastic pieces—only mine would be cast in solid resin. Follow along to see how I built the set.

Figure 5-10 *Using brass forms to mold the classic chess set*

Tools and Materials

I used the following tools to create the brass forms, silicone molds, and resin chess pieces:

- 16" South Bend lathe
- Push knurler
- Bridgeport milling machine
- Indexing head
- Hand files
- Hot glue gun
- Pressure pot
- X-Acto knife
- 1.25" brass stock
- Mold Max 300
- Steel wool

Making the Chess Set

The first step was to carve the pieces out of brass stock. This was rather laborious because I wanted each one to be perfect. I would need to make many molds out of each one, so I wanted them to be durable as well as good-looking. It ended up taking me about one piece a day to design and mill each part. After the brass pieces were done I made molds out of casting silicone and then poured black and white resin to create the set. I'll break down each task in the following steps:

1. Shape the first piece

I put a piece of 1.25" brass stock in my South Bend lathe's three-jaw chuck and simply began free-styling to shape it into a classic chess-piece shape, going off a couple of sketched concepts I had in my mind.

I did the pawn first, because this will establish the style that the other pieces follow. From the neck down the chess pieces mostly look alike. There's a traditional hierarchy of height, which I intended to maintain. I had a cheap set from the five-and-dime that I kept around just to reference.

Once I had carved out the pawn (Figure 5-11), I smoothed it down with a file.

Figure 5-11 *The chess pawn shape emerges from the brass*

2. Make the template

Having established my pawn, I needed to create a template that would allow me to re-create the same curve on the other pieces. I cut a razor blade so that it matched the shape of the neck, and I'll use that while shaping future pieces. I want them all to match!

3. Knurl the base

I used the push-knurler attachment on my lathe to add the cross-hatch pattern (knurling) to the base of the chess piece. You can see both the pattern and the tool in Figure 5-12.

I used the lathe's cutoff tool to cut off the pawn, though I left a lot of stock below the knurling because I'll need to hold on to something when I mold it. Besides, this way I can always put it back into the lathe.

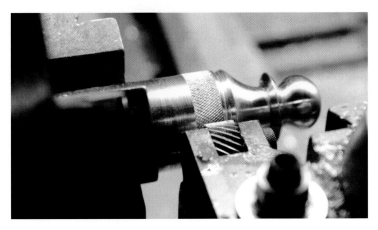

Figure 5-12 *Knurling the base of the pawn*

4. Carve the rook

Next I threw another length of stock in the lathe and began to carve out the rook, or castle. I free-styled the shape as I did with the pawn, then used my razor-blade template to carve the curve to match. Finally, I knurled the base and cut off the rook as I did with the pawn.

I used my Bridgeport milling machine with an indexing head to cut the "battlement" notches in the rook's crown.

5. Make the bishop

By now I was getting very confident with how I wanted the chess set to look, and I grabbed another piece of brass stock and dived right in. I carved out the shape, using the razor blade and steel wool to finish the surface. I knurled and cut off the bishop from the length of brass stock.

As a final step, I put the bishop in my Bridgeport and used the indexing tool to cut the traditional notch (Figure 5-13) in the piece.

Figure 5-13 *Cutting the notch in the bishop*

6. Make the queen

I made the queen next, with it proceeding as expected with the usual curve and collar. It's the second-highest piece in the set, so I measured it out carefully to make sure I was maintaining the hierarchy.

The queen's crown has a number of notches in it, and I used my indexing tool to carve them precisely.

7. Make the king

The king was the biggest challenge up to that point. Hierarchically it is the tallest of the pieces, and as a consequence the piece of stock was jutting pretty far from the lathe's chuck. Working that far from the chuck can be dangerous because the tool sometimes pushes the material off-center. This actually happened to me when working on the king, but fortunately I was able to repair the damage.

I carved, smoothed, and knurled the piece as usual, and then cut it off for finishing in the Bridgeport. I used my indexing tool to carve a cross shape into the peak of the king's crown, as shown in Figure 5-14.

Figure 5-14 *I used the Bridgeport's indexing tool to cut the cross*

8. Make the knight

This is the piece I anticipated would be the most difficult, and so I left it until the end. I made the base of the piece first, with the requisite curvature and knurling.

Then I put the piece in the band saw and basically free-styled a horse shape, cutting the stock flat, then drawing a design on the metal and cutting it into the shape I wanted, using the saw blade to carve into the brass.

Then I worked on it with the hand file, continuing to shape and smooth it into a classic knight. I finished by sanding and buffing it into a smooth sheen. The chess set is done, and you can see it in Figure 5-15. Now to cast them in plastic!

Figure 5-15 *My brass forms are complete*

9. Build the molds

I created eight molds using paper cups glued to sections of junk acrylic sheeting, with a chess piece placed at the bottom. You can see the prepared cups in Figure 5-16.

Then I mixed some Mold Max 30 and poured it into the cups to create the mold.

Figure 5-16 *Making the molds out of paper cups*

10. Finish the molds

I put three cups at a time in my pressure pot, which uses compressed air to force all the bubbles out of the silicone; otherwise, they would show up in the finished pieces. When the molds had hardened, I tore off the paper cups (Figure 5-17) to reveal the rubber mold.

Figure 5-17 *Removing the molds from the paper cups*

11. Cut open the molds

The next step was to cut open the molds and remove the brass forms. I simply cut into the rubber with a X-Acto blade, making a zig-zag cut with my knife. One advantage of using this shape is the molds simply snap back again and reseal. You just cut in enough to remove the object; you don't want to cut the mold in half.

12. Cast the pieces

Having prepared all of the molds, I mixed up some black Smooth-Cast 300 casting resin and started making chess pieces. As with the molds themselves, the castings also had to be put into a pressure pot.

When they had set, I pulled the plastic pieces out of the molds. You can see me inspecting the pieces in Figure 5-18. You may notice there is still an extended base below the knurling, and I sawed off the excess material on my band saw.

Figure 5-18 *The pieces came out of the molds looking great*

13. Finish the set

Having cast all the pieces I needed, I smoothed them all down on the sander and made sure that sat evenly. You can see the nearly finished set in Figure 5-19. Note that there are multiple copies; I made more than one set to ensure I got enough quality pieces.

Figure 5-19 *Nearly finished pieces await their first game*

Summary

I always wanted to do my version of the classic plastic chess set, and I'm really pleased with how it turned out. Next up, I'll make a sign with channel letters formed out of styrene.

Plastic Channel Letters

I made a sign for the champagne brand Freixenet, which needed a branding piece for an event. It was a big logo that would stand on a table. I made the sign using channel letters, which have an inset center and raised edges, making them light up nicely.

With Freixenet, it was more important to maintain the brand's black-and-gold look, so I went with gold-colored LED lights on black letters. Figure 5-20 shows how the sign turned out.

Figure 5-20 *I built this sign out of plastic, MDF, and LED lights*

Tools and Materials

I used the following tools to make my sign:

- ShopBot Desktop
- Band saw
- Welder
- Box cutter
- Chisel
- 1/2" MDF
- Sheet of .040"-thick styrene

- Gold LED lights
- Black spray paint

Building the Letters

The logo consists of a series of cursive letters, milled out of MDF, then lined with 1.5" styrene. LEDs illuminate the channels to make it really pop in a dark room. Read on to learn how I built it:

1. Mill the letter backs

I got the logo vectors from the customer, and laid out a series of boards to be milled on my ShopBot Desktop CNC router, seen in Figure 5-21. I laid it out as big as possible, with the limiting factor being the trademark Freixenet X. I didn't want to cut the X in two, so I'd be limited to a logo size based on the X fitting on a single sheet of MDF. As each shape came off the CNC, I sanded it smooth.

Figure 5-21 *The ShopBot begins to cut the letter shapes*

2. Cut plastic

While the CNC was milling, I cut strips of styrene with a box cutter, making each one about 1-1/4" wide. I chose a thickness of .040" because it was rigid enough to make straight lines, but flexible enough to curve as well. Figure 5-22 shows me cutting the strips.

Figure 5-22 *I began to cut styrene to trim the letters*

4. Glue the X's channels

Next, I started gluing in the styrene to serve as channels. I began with the trademark X and cut a couple of pieces of plastic using a square in order to keep the edges straight.

Originally I was going to use metal for the channels, but I'm glad I didn't. For one thing, it was an interior sign and didn't need that level of durability; and for another, it would just add weight.

Once the strips were the right size, I flexed them to fit the X's curve, then glued them with CA ("super") glue and clamped them into place. CA glue sticks well to both styrene and MDF, though not always instantly—sometimes it takes a few minutes to set. The plastic has a degree of tension and will pop open, particularly if it's curved dramatically, like the pieces shown in Figure 5-23. I also used a CA accelerant that helps the CA to cure more quickly.

Figure 5-23 *Gluing styrene channels to MDF letter shapes*

5. Continue to glue channels

While the channels on the X dried, I worked on the other letters. I was conscious of the thickness of the plastic and cut to ensure that every joint was as neat as possible. If anything, I let the plastic overlap on one side because I'd be sanding it short. When the glue dried, I just cut off that edge. In any case I'm constantly using a square just to make sure everything is clean and straight.

Where there was a serif at the bottom of the letters, I carefully bent the plastic around the curve, as seen in Figure 5-24. As I mentioned earlier in the chapter, it's easy to shape styrene so it will stay curved. I used a pencil and screwdriver as mandrels, or shaping instruments, helping to give the plastic a natural curve.

People asked why I didn't heat up the plastic to make it bend better. When I bend the plastic around a mandrel, it bends the way I want; but when I heat up the styrene, it basically becomes a wet noodle and there's no way to control it. There's no reason to heat when you use the right thickness of styrene.

Figure 5-24 *Gluing channels onto the letter shapes*

6. Cut off the overlaps

While I waited for glue to dry, I took the finished channels to the band saw and cut off the overlaps as shown in Figure 5-25. Where there were overlaps inside the letters and I couldn't saw them, I trimmed the edges with a sharp chisel.

Figure 5-25 *Trimming off the overlaps on the band saw*

7. Smooth down the edges

The band saw left some rough edges, so I went over the channels with my file, then sanded them down with sandpaper. While the plastic will be painted, and in any event will be in a darkened room, I still wanted them as smooth as possible. Figure 5-26 shows me smoothing down the burrs.

Figure 5-26 *Using a flat file to smooth down the sawn edges of the styrene*

8. Paint the letters

I sprayed down the letters with black spray paint. Paint works with styrene beautifully, covering up cracks and joins while not distracting from the smoothness of the plastic. I made a mistake in this sign, and should have painted the insides of the letters gold. My gut instinct was to make them gold, and after I was done I wished I had—it would have given the letters a nice pop. Figure 5-27 shows the painted sign.

Figure 5-27 *The letters with a couple coats of black spray paint*

9. Drill the light-holes

Once the paint was dry, I brought the letters to the drill press (Figure 5-28) and drilled a series of holes for the LEDs. I just eyeballed the spacing, because no one will know or care that they're not spaced with mathematical perfection.

Figure 5-28 *Drilling LED holes in the letters*

10. Add the lights

The sign will be sitting on a table at a party, so I wanted the customer to be able to turn the lights on even if there wasn't an outlet nearby. Therefore, I decided to use battery-powered lights, and I found strands of 20 with a light gold coloration, which matched Freixenet's branding.

I added a few sets of battery-powered, gold-colored LED lights, shown in Figure 5-29. I inserted each LED into one of the holes I drilled, then taped and hot-glued it in place. I ended up needing six battery packs. They were pre-arranged in a strand, and I knew I'd waste some LEDs and have to cover them up.

I also had to have some wires crossing between letters, making the wires visible from the front, but since I knew the sign would be in a darkened room, I didn't sweat it too much.

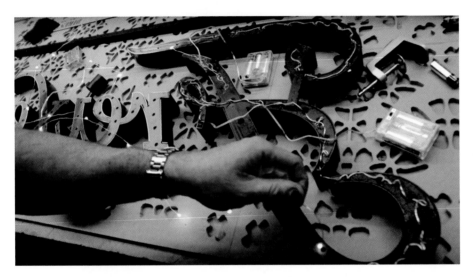

Figure 5-29 *The sign ended up using six strands of gold LEDs*

11. Attach the letters together

I grabbed some wooden struts, painted black to match the channels, to attach all the letter sections together to maintain the correct letter spacing. I used hot glue and screws to bolt everything together, with a single wooden bar (seen in Figure 5-30) doing most of the support. This bar has a couple of drilled holes into which the metal stand's vertical struts will get inserted.

Figure 5-30 *Attaching the letters to a wooden support bar*

12. Color the channel edges

I realized the sign wasn't popping as much as I wanted, so I used a gold paint marker to color in the edges of the channels. Figure 5-31 shows me nearly finished with the project.

Figure 5-31 *Coloring in the channel edges with a gold paint marker*

13. Make the stand

The sign will be positioned on a tabletop stand, so I cut lengths of steel, forming a basic frame that will support the sign. After welding the steel together (Figure 5-32), I used a grinder to polish down the frame, then spray-painted it to match the rest. The sign slips right onto the top of the stand, making for quick assembly. It's done!

Figure 5-32 *Welding together lengths of steel to create a frame*

Summary

Combining CNC-milled MDF with plastic channels made for a great sign, and it was a fun project. That brings Chapter 5 to a close! I really enjoy working with plastic and I hope you do too.

Working with Leather §

Along with wood, leather represents one of humanity's earliest building materials. I've done a lot of work with leather, whether making sheaths and cases for my various tools, making an embossed wallet, or even sewing a pair of leather pants, seen in Figure 6-1.

In this chapter I'll share a selection of some of my favorite leather-working tools as well as a pair of projects: a knife sheath and a backpack.

Figure 6-1 *I reinforced a pair of jeans with leather*

Leather Tools and Materials

Leather has a unique set of tools to cut, shape, and emboss it. These are tools I use the most when working with leather.

Arbor Press

I mostly use my arbor press, also known as a 12-ton press, for impressing leather and book covers. You can see the press at work in Figure 6-2. I bought it on a lark from Harbor Freight, not really knowing what I would do with it, but once I got it I totally started inventing purposes for it. I really couldn't live without this in the shop, now that I've used it for so many small things.

Figure 6-2 *Embossing leather with an arbor press*

Awl

I often need a sharp piercing thing to use when working with leather. An awl is simply a heavy needle for piercing things. I usually use my own ice pick (pictured in Figure 6-3 and described in Chapter 7) in place of an awl when working in leather and pretty much all of the time. It's good for lining up stitching holes, making punctures, and scratching guide marks in the leather.

Figure 6-3 *I use my ice pick for many different uses—including as an awl*

Branding Iron

I like to add my logo to all of my projects, and when it comes to leather, the best way to do it involves a branding iron, seen in Figure 6-4. I'm literally branding my projects as being my creations! I use a branding iron made by a friend, and simply heat it up with a propane torch to get it hot enough to scorch the leather.

Figure 6-4 *Branding a leather axe sheath with my branding iron*

Jade Glue

I use jade glue (Figure 6-5) in my leather projects. Intended as a bookbinder's glue, PVA or jade glue is archival, meaning it doesn't yellow and crack as it gets old. However, I often use other kinds of glue like CA glue and 3M spray adhesive. A lot of leatherworkers use Barge Cement, a two-coat rubber cement. Mostly I just use glue to hold pieces of leather in place before I even stitch them.

Figure 6-5 *PVA, or jade glue, works great for attaching two pieces of leather*

Juki Serger

The Juki (seen in Figure 6-6) is an industrial-strength sewing machine able to sew through leather. Juki makes many different models of sewing machines with a million features, but I like the one I have because it's very simple and very powerful.

Figure 6-6 *Sewing leather into denim with a Juki serger*

Mallet

I use a mallet (Figure 6-7) to pound various embossing tools and for other reasons. I made my own mallet, but any typical wooden mallet will work. However, I don't just limit myself to this one; I also use a brass hammer to tap on stitching forks and the like.

Figure 6-7 *You'd be surprised how often a mallet comes in handy*

Needles and Thread

As great as the Juki might be, oftentimes I find myself sewing by hand. I keep a supply of leather-gauge needles and waxed nylon thread (Figure 6-8) on hand. The thread I use is so strong I can't break it by hand; I keep it around in black and white.

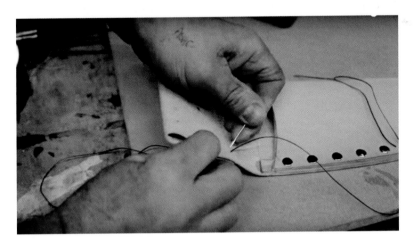

Figure 6-8 *Sewing leather with a needle and thread*

Punch

To make holes in leather, you can't just shove an awl through; the material just closes up again. The solution is a punch (Figure 6-9), which actually removes material rather than shoving it aside. Leather punches often have multiple diameters available, allowing you to make the perfect hole.

Figure 6-9 *Hole punches cut a hole in the leather*

Rivet, Snap, and Grommet Stampers

These are small tools for attaching grommets, snaps, studs, and rivets to leather. A stamper looks vaguely like a bullet (Figure 6-10) and is used in conjunction with a hammer to force the front and back of each part together. Typically each set comes with a bottom and top die, as well as a hole punch for making the right-sized hole in the material.

Figure 6-10 *The rivet stamper helps you set these small pieces of hardware*

Skiver

When I need to make thick leather thinner, I use a skiver to scrape away unwanted material. These tools resemble small knives and come in a variety of configurations depending on the use; the one seen in Figure 6-11 is meant for beveling the edge of the leather.

Figure 6-11 *I use small knives to skive away unwanted leather*

Stitching Fork

This tool helps space out stitching holes so they look neat and orderly. You simply stamp it once, then put one or more of the tines into the holes you already made so that the spacing remains perfect.

I have several different forks, including some for punching holes at angles and some for straight holes. Forks also come in different numbers of teeth, and this gives you the flexibility to make stitches in smaller and larger pieces of leather.

Typically I can punch through two layers of leather with my forks, and if I have more layers to go through, I switch to a drill press. Figure 6-12 shows me using a stitching fork.

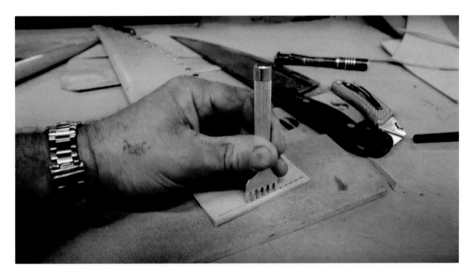

Figure 6-12 *Using a stitching fork to space out the holes*

X-Acto Knife

I usually use my trusty box cutter to cut leather, but it isn't a very precise instrument. For finer work I use an X-Acto knife (Figure 6-13) constantly for cutting out, carving, and skiving. One thing I like about these knives is that if it gets dull, you just get a new one. A lot of leatherworking is steeped in traditional tools and methods and people want to buy a special tool and then sharpen it all the time. I can see the advantages, but I like to use disposable blades and simply swap them out when they get dull.

Figure 6-13 *I use an X-Acto knife for smaller cuts*

Big-Ass Knife Sheath Project

I made a Big-Ass Knife out of a lumber mill saw blade that had been rusting for 50 years on my property in upstate New York. It was really big and really sharp and it really needed a sheath, so I made one. You can see what I came up with in Figure 6-14. Read on to learn how I created it.

Figure 6-14 *This leather shield keeps my Big-Ass Knife safe and secure*

Tools and Materials

The sheath was deceptively simple and only used a few tools:

- 8 oz vegetable-tanned leather
- Box cutter
- Drill press
- Needle and thread
- PVA glue
- Rivets, setting tool, and mallet
- Branding iron and propane torch

Making the Sheath

I followed these steps in creating my sheath:

1. Cut the leather

I found the perfect piece of leather to turn into a sheath. I traced the knife (Figure 6-15) and used a box cutter to cut out a piece of leather that matches the blade. It doesn't need to be perfect because I'll just smooth it down later.

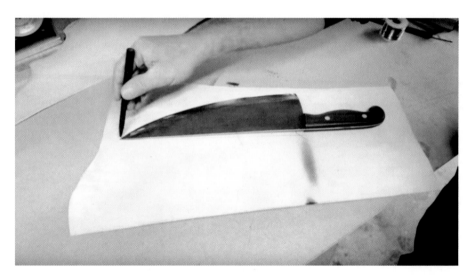

Figure 6-15 *Tracing the knife blade*

2. Add the welting

I added welting, a reinforcing strip of leather (Figure 6-16) where the blade will touch. This keeps the edge from cutting into the seam. I'm just gluing the welting in place for now; I'll rivet it later to secure it properly.

Figure 6-16 *Gluing in the welting*

3. Fold and shape the sheath

Having traced the leather, I cut it into a close approximation (seen in Figure 6-17) of how the final sheath would look.

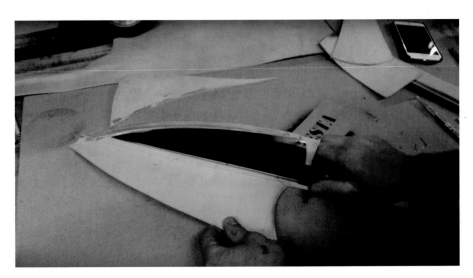

Figure 6-17 *Cutting the final sheath shape*

4. Glue the flap

I glued the sheath and held it in place (Figure 6-18) until the glue set, not bothering to clamp it. The glue is just there to keep it in place for the rivets, which will do the actual attaching.

Once the glue had cured, I took the sheath to my belt sander and smoothed down the uneven parts.

Figure 6-18 *Gluing the sheath*

5. Drill rivet holes

A lot of time people use punches to make holes in leather, but oftentimes I prefer to use a drill press because it's faster and easier. On soft, floppy material it would never work, but for multilayer, glued leather like this, a drill works well. I spaced out rivet holes using a compass, then drilled.

6. Add rivets

I added rivets and rivet washers to each hole, then secured them with a rivet setting tool and hammer.

7. Make the belt loop

Next, I wanted to add a belt loop. I left excess material at the top, so I trimmed what was left and folded it over.

8. Stitch the belt loop

Using a stitching fork, I punched thread holes in the leather, then glued the flap into place. With the flap fixed, I used my stitching fork again to ensure the holes went all the way through. After all that was done, I stitched the flap. You can see me sewing in Figure 6-19.

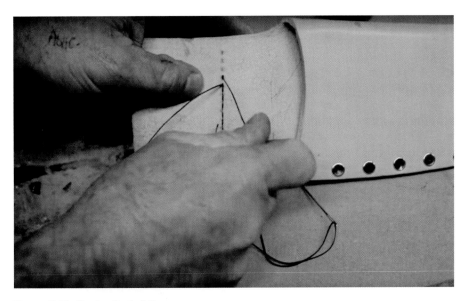

Figure 6-19 *Sewing the belt flap*

9. Brand the leather

I grabbed a branding iron my friend Tony made for me, heated it up with a propane torch, then branded the leather. You can see how it turned out in Figure 6-20.

Figure 6-20 *Putting the finishing touches on the sheath*

Summary

Most of my projects have a very real reason for existing. In the case of this sheath, I just wanted something to protect the knife from damage, while keeping the edge away from my skin. I'm very happy with how the sheath turned out. Next up, I'll show you how I designed and assembled my own backpack.

Adirondack-Style Leather Backpack

My inspiration for this project is the Adirondack backpack. Often you'll see them made out of wicker and they're essentially a dump bin for your back. My backpack (Figure 6-21), rather than wicker, uses vegetable-tanned leather to form the body. It has a brass latch I built myself and can be converted from a backpack to a shoulder bag.

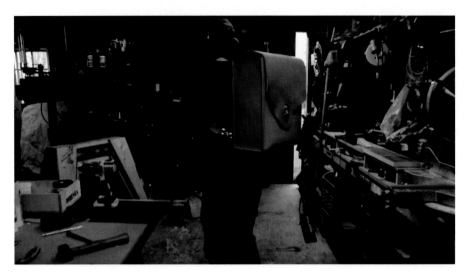

Figure 6-21 *Trying on my new backpack*

Tools and Materials

I used the following tools and materials in creating my backpack:

- Wood for wet-forming leather
- 8 oz vegetable-tanned leather
- PVA glue
- Stitching fork
- Brass hardware
- Brass lanyards
- Silver solder and propane torch

Making the Backpack

I'm very pleased with how my backpack turned out. Here's how I made it:

1. Build the form

I began the project by building wooden forms (Figure 6-22) that will shape the sides of the backpack. The forms consist of a piece of smooth, finished plywood with a frame on three sides. When I push the leather into one of these forms, it will give the material sort of a "lip" on three sides.

Figure 6-22 *Making the forms*

2. Rough-cut the side pieces

I measured out the sides and rough-cut (Figure 6-23) the leather. I'll trim it closer later on. In the meantime, however, I need extra material around the edge for when I put the leather in the form.

Figure 6-23 *Rough-cutting the sides of the backpack*

3. Put the leather in the form

I soaked the side pieces in hot water until they were soft and pliable. Then I put both pieces into the forms (Figure 6-24), clamping them securely.

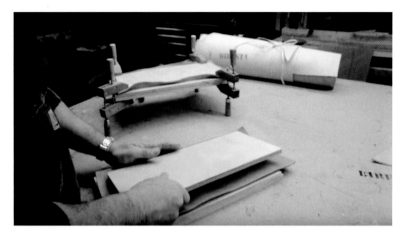

Figure 6-24 *Putting the softened leather in a wooden form*

4. Cut off the rough edges

Once the leather had set, I trimmed off the rough edges (Figure 6-25) with my box cutter, using the form itself as a guide for my knife. The side portions ended up with only a quarter inch of space for a single row of stitching. Next time I'll leave half an inch and double-stitch.

Figure 6-25 *Cutting off the excess leather*

5. Cut the leather for the body

Next, I cut the leather for the back, bottom, and front, seen in Figure 6-26. I didn't have enough material to make a flap as well, so I trimmed it off with a couple inches left over so I can add a flap later.

Figure 6-26 *Cutting the leather for the back, bottom, and front of the backpack*

6. Construct a wooden box

I made a wooden box (Figure 6-27) for the body of the pack, with blue painter's tape protecting any surface that might come in contact with the glue. The purpose of the box is to keep the backpack's volume and shape even while I sew.

Figure 6-27 *Building a wooden box to keep the backpack steady while I sew its seams*

7. Glue and clamp the leather

Once the box was complete, I wrapped the big piece of leather around it, gluing the sides on and clamping everything. Figure 6-28 shows one seam getting clamped.

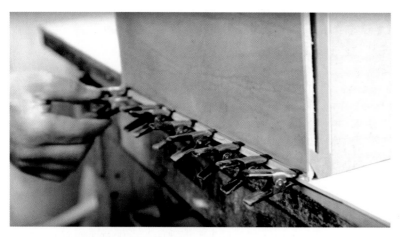

Figure 6-28 *Gluing and clamping a seam*

8. Make the stitching holes

When the glue was dry, the clamps came off. However, I didn't remove the box yet. First I wanted to sew up the seams. Before I could do that, however, I'd need stitching holes, so I worked my way around the seams with my stitching fork.

9. Sew the seams

When all the stitching holes had been made, I sewed them using waxed nylon thread and a needle. Figure 6-29 shows me sewing a side panel, literally going in and out of every hole.

Figure 6-29 *Sewing the seams with waxed thread*

10. Smooth the edges

With the glue dry and the seams sewed, my work was nearly done. One thing I wanted to do was smooth down the seams, which were a little uneven. I used a hand plane (Figure 6-30) to smooth down the rough edges, and it worked perfectly.

Figure 6-30 *Surprisingly, leather planes just as well as wood!*

11. Cut the flap

With the box still inside the backpack, I cut a piece of leather for the flap. I wanted some of the natural edging, so I used a piece close to the edge of the hide.

12. Attach the flap

I glued the flap in place, clamped the join, then sewed a double row of stitches to secure it. You can see me sewing in Figure 6-31.

Figure 6-31 *Gluing and sewing the flap*

13. Reinforce the top

I removed the wooden box and glued in some strips of oak to reinforce the top of the bag so it doesn't become shapeless.

14. Build the hardware

With the main pack done, I switched things up and worked on the brass hardware. I made my own, cutting plates of brass and soldering on rings, as seen in Figure 6-32. I made a closure mechanism, a reinforcing plate, and a backplate, along with rings for attaching the shoulder straps.

Figure 6-32 *Making brass hardware out of stock*

15. Attach the hardware

I attached the closure mechanism, riveting the plate onto the leather with the help of a back plate. Figure 6-33 shows the mechanism getting placed.

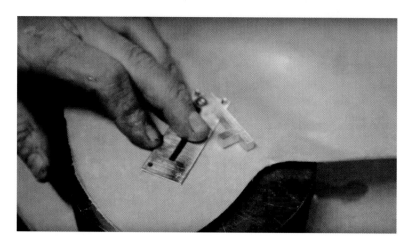

Figure 6-33 *Attaching the closure mechanism*

16. Make the shoulder straps

I cut shoulder straps, then glued and sewed them into place. Figure 6-34 shows the straps partially done.

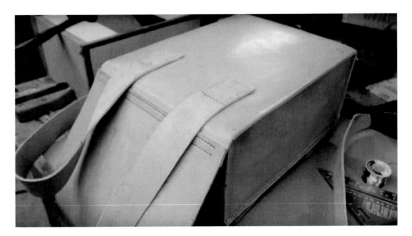

Figure 6-34 *Sewing on shoulder straps*

17. Add swivel snap hooks

I sewed swivel snap hooks (Figure 6-35) onto the bottoms of the shoulder straps. I got them from a horse supply company, and they'll work perfectly to keep the straps in check.

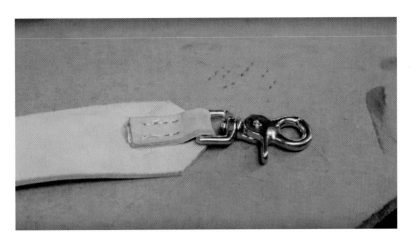

Figure 6-35 *Swivel snap hooks attach the bottoms of the shoulder straps to the bag*

18. Install grommets

I added a pair of brass grommets and a removable carrying handle for when I didn't want the pack on my back. I'm done!

Summary

The backpack is done! It will definitely get used and my only worry is that the single stitching on the sides won't prove enough—I'm kicking myself for not leaving more leather sticking out of my forms. However, this was the very first leather bag I made, and I learned a lot during the process, so I'm not worried.

Chapter 7 finishes off the book with a discussion of my favorite topic: tools! I love to build my own tools and to modify existing ones to work better for me, and I'll share some of my favorites.

Building Your Own Tools 7

I love using tools, but also making them, restoring old ones, and modifying them to work better. There are so many tools in my workshop that I have made better in some way. In some cases I'll take an unwanted old tool and make it completely different, like the machete project from Chapter 2. In other cases, I combine two tools into one, like the Which Blade 1 seen in Figure 7-1.

Figure 7-1 *The Which Blade 1 mashes up a fixed-blade knife and a multitool*

In this chapter I'll share some of my favorite modified tools, and then will guide you step by step through five fun projects: creating an aluminum handle for an axe, making a locket with three keys attached to it, constructing a brass-ringed wooden mallet, making a wavy-bladed kris knife, and cranking out a production run of a hundred ice picks.

Gallery of Modified Tools

The following are some of my favorite created or modified tools.

Buck Auto-Knife

I converted a classic Buck knife (seen in Figure 7-2) into an auto-knife—a "switchblade"—by adding a length of steel harvested from an old spring, along with a button to keep it in place. I made a couple of mistakes in the build that resulted in the knife being ruined, but I plan on revamping my design and making another go of it.

Figure 7-2 *This project adds a button and a stronger spring to a regular Buck knife*

Bottle Openers

One of my videos features 12 bottle openers repurposed from other tools: a putty knife, an old wrench, and so on. One of the variants was a chisel equipped with a cap-lifting tongue (seen in Figure 7-3) thanks to my drill press. Another consisted of a long screwdriver whose driving end was twisted into a bottle-lifter.

Figure 7-3 *I made a dozen bottle openers using different repurposed tools*

Chisel Makeover

I restored an old chisel (Figure 7-4) by patching up its broken end using my welder, sanding down the rough edges with my Beaumont belt sender, then sharpening the chisel on my Veritas Mk. II knife sharpener. I finished off the project with a lovely brass handle I turned on my lathe.

Figure 7-4 *I restored this old chisel and added a brass handle*

Dagger from File

This is another project involving converting one tool to another. I was inspired by a trip to the Pittsburgh Maker Faire, where I met an artist making his own knives, including ones ground out of old files. I had an old file and I decided that I wanted to turn it into a medieval-style dagger.

First I heated the file in my forge to remove the temper, then ground a point onto the end of it. Next I beveled the blade using my Bridgeport vertical mill, then smoothed down the bevels on the belt sander. I made the bottom part of the file into the hilt of the dagger, giving it a nice knurled grip. I originally intended to wrap the handle in leather, but I liked the old file pattern so much I kept it.

I re-tempered the blade in my forge and quenched it in oil, then made a black leather sheath that matched the dark steel. You can see the finished dagger in Figure 7-5.

Figure 7-5 *I ground a dagger out of an old file*

Estwing Hatchet

Estwing makes some lovely hatchets, and their distinctive leather handles make them stand out from the competition. However, that organic handle is always the first part of the hatchet to deteriorate. I took an old Estwing with a corroded head and rotten handle and refurbished it, cutting off the old leather and replacing it with a polished padauk-wood handle. I even braided my own leather lanyard. You can see the finished hatchet in Figure 7-6.

Figure 7-6 *This Estwing hatchet has a new padauk-wood handle*

Fireman's Axe

Another axe project! I restored a classic True Temper Kelly Standard pick-head axe that was missing its handle. I restored the head first, sandblasting off the corrosion and then polishing up the metal with my grinder and palm sander.

To shape the point where the handle goes into the head, I filled it with Mold Max castable rubber, giving me a very accurate sense of the shape I needed to make the ash handle. The head, meanwhile, was sent out to Performance Plating in Kansas City to be covered in chrome. Finally, and like a lot of my bladed projects, I took the time to build a black leather sheath, seen in Figure 7-7. Thanks to Tracy for donating the axe head and handle blank!

Figure 7-7 *This fireman's axe sports a chrome-plated head and blackened ash handle*

Hammer Hook and Loop

I needed a hammer for use up on a ladder. Some pants come with a hammer loop, but you can't count on that! I welded a hook right on the handle of an Estwing hammer, positioning the hardware in such a way that it would be ready for use when I grabbed it. I also added a loop where I could tie a cord around the hammer, so I wouldn't drop it off the ladder. You can see the hammer in Figure 7-8.

Figure 7-8 *Adding a hook and loop onto the end of a regular hammer*

Kitchen Knife

I made my own kitchen knife, seen in Figure 7-9. I bought a piece of O-1 oil-hardening tooling steel, ground it into a knife shape, then beveled the cutting edge by clamping it to a plank with a 5% angle and then sliding the assembly past my belt sander. The extra-long handle is made out of Madagascar ebony.

I use this knife all the time in the kitchen, and it's starting to get a little stained, but it's still sharp. I plan on making a whole set of kitchen knives.

Figure 7-9 *I ground a kitchen knife out of a piece of tooling steel*

Leatherman Clip

I love my Leatherman tool; I hate the belt case that came with it. My solution was to TIG-weld a 3/16" stainless steel loop (seen in Figure 7-10) so I could hang it from my belt. The loop attaches to both handles of the multitool, which ordinarily would prevent it from opening up. My solution was to split the loop in two.

Figure 7-10 *Forget belt sheaths; I welded a clip onto mine*

Steel Sawhorses

I just got a new welder and needed a project to test it out, so I decided to build a set of steel sawhorses.

I cut eight identical lengths of steel stock, then used my band saw to cut identical notches in the end to ensure they're angled right. Those notches connected to more lengths of square stock, forming four identical frames of metal. I joined them together with heavy-duty hinges. I ended up with some way-strong sawhorses (seen in Figure 7-11) that are likely to be tougher than any use I'll come up with.

One of my YouTube commenters said he built a pair of similar steel sawhorses that together held almost 45,000 pounds before they bent. They may not be the strongest in the world, but they're definitely stronger than the wood sawhorses I own.

Figure 7-11 *Welded steel sawhorses ready for my toughest job*

Two-Claw Hammer

For this project, I took an ordinary Estwing claw hammer and welded a crowbar claw onto it, oriented 90 degrees off the other one. I essentially took a crowbar and cut it in half, and added a claw-hammer head. You can see what I came up with in Figure 7-12.

Figure 7-12 *I mashed up a crowbar and a claw hammer*

The Which Blade

I already mentioned the Which Blade. So there are two variants of a simple idea: using a Leatherman multitool as the handle for another knife. The first blade consisted of a skeleton hand fused to a knife blade, with the hand serving as a holder for the Leatherman. The second Which Blade, seen in Figure 7-13, has a removable fixed blade and uses the Leatherman itself as the handle.

Figure 7-13 *The Which Blade 2 features a fixed blade with a multitool handle*

Summary

Those were some overviews of modified tools. Now let's delve into five other builds, and I'll show you how I created each one.

Bringing an Old Axe Back to Life

I got this double-bitted "Lakeside" axe at a garage sale for 10 bucks, and it's been hanging in my garage in upstate New York ever since. The axe head is old and rusty, with a broken handle sticking out of it. I always intended to remake the handle, and kept the old stump around so I'd have a really nice pattern for the inside of the head.

After I finished restoring the axe (Figure 7-14) I built a cigar-box-like case for the head out of wood and leather, and it even has a small file stored in the case if I need to sharpen the blade.

Figure 7-14 *This axe needed a new handle, so I created one out of a block of aluminum*

Tools and Materials

I used the following power tools in my project:

- Band saw
- Beaumont belt sander
- Buffer
- Die grinder
- Dremel with Roto-Zip bit
- Drill press
- Palm sander
- Benchtop sandblaster
- Table saw

I also used the following hand tools and materials:

- Angle finder
- Brass hammer
- Ball peen hammer
- Digital caliper
- Files (flat, bastard)
- Permanent marker
- Quick Cure five-minute epoxy
- PVA bookbinder's glue
- West System epoxy
- West System filleting blend #405

Restoring the Axe

The essence of this project is to cut a plausible axe handle out of a block of aluminum, then smooth it down with saws, files, sanders, and other polishing and cutting devices until it's just as smooth and comfortable as a "real" handle. This is what I did to build mine:

1. Clean up the head

It's difficult to work with a dirty tool, so as a first step, I burnished off all the rust and dirt using my benchtop sandblaster. It leaves a dull finish that is a perfect starting point for a restoration and, as the project progressed, I eventually gave it a very nice sheen.

2. Remove the handle

Next I removed what's left of the handle, while damaging it as little as possible. The handle stump is secured to the head with a steel wedge that splits the handle in half and forces it to press up against the axe head. I used a Dremel rotary tool with a Roto-Zip bit to dig into the wood around the wedge, though it turned out to be very old and dry, and the wedge came out rather quickly.

As soon as the wedge came out, the handle stump pretty much came right off, revealing the exact shape I need to replicate in my aluminum handle. It was interesting seeing the original tooling marks on the handle (Figure 7-15) from when the axe was new, however many years ago!

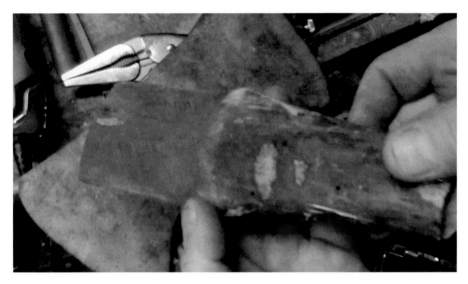

Figure 7-15 *The handle's stump gave me a perfect model for the new handle*

3. Design the new handle

I found a piece of general-purpose 6160 aluminum that would form the new handle. It was much heavier than I expected, even though I ended up cutting away 30–40% of the material. First I traced the profile of the old handle (Figure 7-16). Then I drew out the axe handle on the aluminum using a permanent marker. Everyone was impressed that I draw the handle freehand, but I just used the edge of the metal as a guide, holding my fingers to keep the pen steady.

Figure 7-16 *Using a permanent marker to draw the shape of the handle on the aluminum*

4. Cut the aluminum

I cut out the design on my band saw using a 4 tooth-per-inch (TPI) blade, as seen in Figure 7-17. The metal tends to get gummy, and if you use a typical metal-cutting blade (say, 14 TPI) the metal shavings don't fall out of the blade and it gets gummed up.

I cut out the left and right sides, then flipped the metal 90 degrees and cut down the sides as well, to give it the beginnings of sort of a taper. I'm basically scalloping out all four sides.

Figure 7-17 *Cutting out the design from a block of aluminum*

After that I worked on the shoulder, the part of the handle that fits into the axe head. This presented something of a challenge, as I had to drop the shape on the end of the handle and you cut on a band saw by pushing the material into the blade. This means I couldn't see the line, so I set up my camera to shoot the video and followed along with the lines on the camera's viewfinder. I angled the material as I shoved it through the saw blade to give it a beveled edge roughly analogous to the socket of the axe head.

After I shaped the shoulder, I beveled the edges of the main handle (Figure 7-18), trying to keep my hands steady so there wouldn't be any unevenness. I just kept cutting down corners, working off all those facets until I started having a round shape that would fit well in my hand. This technique isn't perfect, but it's a lot easier using the saw than working it by hand. Don't work too quickly—just take little bits out at a time.

Figure 7-18 *I continued to bevel the edges with the band saw*

5. Smooth the handle

Once the facets had been cut off as much as possible, the hard work began. I worked over the handle with the lead file some more and used the flexible part of my Beaumont belt sander to help round the edges. I used a pretty aggressive belt on the Beaumont, 80-50— any less and the grit gets gummy.

Next, I worked the handle over with a bastard file. It's got flat and curved sides, and you'll need both when making this kind of handle. I found I could really see the blade marks on the handle. Just when I thought I had them all off, I found more. I ended up using a really aggressive rasp because I wasn't getting enough material off.

I repeatedly measured the widths with my digital caliper to ensure that the final shape would be even. Then I worked over the handle with the Belmont sander (Figure 7-19), my air-powered die grinder, as well as a palm sander. Just work your way down the grits, and you can pretty much get anything shiny.

Figure 7-19 *I switched to the Belmont sander*

6. Add the head

The first step to adding the head is to cut a slot into the shoulder, giving the hand end a degree of flexibility. You'll eventually add a brass wedge, which will ensure the axe head doesn't fall off.

At this time I polished up the head (Figure 7-20), but I didn't overdo it. I liked the wear on the steel from decades of use, and anyway I knew the handle would be shiny, so I left the axe head a little more rough and worn.

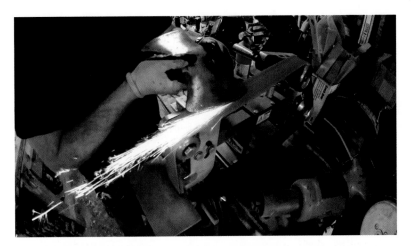

Figure 7-20 *Polishing up the axe head just before adding it to the handle*

I tapped on the end of the axe handle, inserting the handle into the opening incrementally with every tap. I left enough material sticking out of the top of the head to sand off once the wedge is placed.

7. Add the wedge

When the head was firmly attached, I cut out a piece of brass and shaped it into a wedge on the belt sander. I inserted the wedge and pounded it as far as it would go, then sanded off the excess. Finally, I pounded on the end with a ball peen hammer, just to give it some texture. The axe is done!

8. Build the case edges

Every sharp tool needs a sheath or protective case, and my axe was no different. I cut some walnut panels with finger-jointed ends, and came up with the idea of a case resembling a cigar box to enclose the axe's head.

Once I had formed the shape I wanted, I added Quick Cure epoxy to the dovetails, then arranged the pieces by hand, as seen in Figure 7-21. I sanded the edges smooth once the epoxy had set, and filled in the excess holes in the dovetail arrangement with West System filleting blend, wood-toned filler that mixes with epoxy.

Figure 7-21 *I epoxied the dovetailed segments and arranged them by hand*

9. Add leather

I had some heavy-duty cowhide from a previous project, and I traced out the head's shape onto the leather (Figure 7-22), then cut it out roughly with my box cutter. I glued the leather onto the frame with PVA, then trimmed carefully around the edge with an X-Acto knife.

Figure 7-22 *Tracing out the shape of the case*

10. Finish the case

I cut the case in half. I set up my table saw for the width I wanted (halfway through the case) and rotated the case over the saw blade, eventually cutting it in half. I was very careful to go slow so the blade didn't grab the case. I made a bunch of passes, rotating the box frequently.

Once I cut the case open, I added small pieces of wood to help keep the axe head from moving around. Next, I secured the leather parts of the case by pre-drilling holes for small brass tacks, then tapped them in with a finishing hammer. After that I added hinges and locking mechanisms, screwing them in place. I didn't have mirrored locks, so I rotated one 180 degrees, making one lock opposite the other, meaning the case doesn't really have a top or bottom. Figure 7-23 shows the final case.

Figure 7-23 *Adding a file so the axe can be sharpened in the field*

11. Sharpen and use

I sharpened the axe and brought it up to my property in upstate New York, and put it to work by cutting down a dead tree. People ask how comfortable it is to use. It cuts as smooth as you'd like, but it's heavy!

Summary

This project demonstrates that even an old and rusty axe with a broken handle can be made useful again. All it takes is a lot of hard work and, in the case of this project, a big piece of aluminum!

Making a Star Key Locket

About 20 years ago I decided the sound of jangling keys was annoying to me. I decided to come up with a solution that would let me carry several keys without the noise. The first thing I tried was to put a screw through the holes in the keys, and then simply fanning them out when I needed to unlock something. One day I was fanning them out and realized they looked really cool in a star formation.

To make a star key I soldered the keys to a central hub, almost like a pocket watch (you can see several variations in Figure 7-24). It also got a lot skinnier. Where before it was almost like a pocket knife, a lump in my front pocket, now it's just a flat key that hangs from my belt or goes into my billfold. Every time I move into a new space I end up creating a new key. Sometimes they're simpler, like a brass lanyard with a single key soldered to it, but sometimes they're more complicated.

Figure 7-24 *Star keys are just the ticket if you don't like jangling in your pocket*

A friend wanted a star key made into a locket, and gave me a vintage button to use. It's a big brass button that I was going to turn into a locket, with the keys soldered around the periphery.

Tools and Materials

While small, the key project uses a wide variety of tools and materials:

- Beaumont belt sander
- Button
- Brass rod a little bit wider than the button
- Caliper
- Cutting fluid
- Dremel
- Drill press
- Jeweler's saw
- Keys
- Lathe
- Propane torch
- Silver solder
- Ultra Flux
- Wire brush

Assembling the Locket

Here are the steps I took in creating my star key. The main design involves the antique button (Figure 7-25) that my friend supplied.

Figure 7-25 *This button will serve as the front of the locket*

1. Shape the locket backing

The first step is to find a piece of brass that will serve as the back of the locket. Naturally, it's got to match the diameter of the front. I grabbed a piece of brass rod that a friend saved for me from a recycling plant. A short length of this material will eventually turn into the back of the locket after I run it through the lathe.

I cut off a length of the brass rod and secured it to my lathe. Boring into the end, I cut out a small hollow for the inside of the locket. I used my internal caliper occasionally to make sure I was making the hollow the right size.

2. Clean up the button

Next, I worked on preparing the button. It consisted of a brass cover attached to a backing, with paper batting inside. I used a Dremel and saw bit to cut out the back of the button.

Next, I used an ice pick to clear that paper batting out and then removed the remainder of the backing. I worked really gently because I didn't want to deform the front of the button, because if it gets deformed it's garbage.

I tested the button face in the hollowed-out portion of the rod, and when I confirmed it fit, it was time to cut off the locket backing from the rod.

3. Cut off and clean up the backing

I used a lathe's parting tool (seen in Figure 7-26) to cut into the rod, while simultaneously making an extra groove for the keys to go into.

Figure 7-26 *Cutting through the brass with a parting tool*

I went as deep as I could with the parting tool, then cut off the remainder with a hacksaw. The piece of brass was just too close to the lathe's three-jaw chuck to cut all the way through with the parting tool.

When the locket backing came off the rod, I cleaned up the back with the sander, dipping it into a cup of water periodically so it wouldn't get too hot to hold.

4. Build the hardware

I needed to create all-new hardware for the locket—a hinge, as well as a lever to help open it. I used a jeweler's saw to cut out a small piece of brass for the lever. This will give the user's finger something to grab ahold of when opening the locket.

I used silver solder to attach the lever to the locket face. First, I threw some flux on the area I wanted to solder, along with some flakes of silver, and then I heated it up with a propane torch. Since the brass button face is so thin, I had a piece of metal underneath, and I directed the torch on this (as seen in Figure 7-27) to avoid overheating the brass. This project was a challenge for me because I'm not used to working tiny!

Figure 7-27 *Heating up a piece of metal to melt solder*

Next, I worked on the hinge. I used my jeweler's saw to cut out tiny lengths of brass tubing and soldered them onto the locket front and backing. Then I attached the two tubes to the backing, using the hinge pin to keep them aligned.

Unfortunately, while soldering everything into place I soldered the hinge pin, so I had to heat it up red-hot and remove it, as seen in Figure 7-28. For the most part, silver solder is very controllable and it's easy to pinpoint what you want to get hot and what you don't.

It also helps to work on steel blocks, positioned to serve as heat sinks for the parts of the locket I don't want to get hot. Once I had the hinge the way I wanted it, I re-inserted the hinge pin and sanded off the extra portion.

Figure 7-28 *Soldering hinge tubes to the locket back. The larger piece of brass holds the tubes in place.*

5. Solder in the keys

Then it was time to add the three keys. First, I cut off the backs of the keys. Next, I inserted the first key into that groove in the side of the locket back, then coated the end in flux.

Figure 7-29 shows the first key in place. Notice how I positioned the key so it was cantilevered between two steel blocks, essentially excluding that part of the locket from the heat sink.

Figure 7-29 *Arranging the keys with steel blocks underneath to serve as heat sinks*

Then I heated the brass with the torch while applying a length of silver solder. I worked my way around and soldered in all three keys. I covered the hinge with a steel plate to avoid re-activating the solder and knocking those hinge tubes out of position.

After I'd soldered in all three keys, I quenched the locket in a cup of water and cleaned it up with a brass wire brush in a drill press. When it was clean, I stamped my name in the inside.

My friend wanted the star key on a lanyard, so I drilled a hole in one of the keys and added a jump ring. It's done! Figure 7-30 shows the completed project.

Figure 7-30 *The finished star key locket, along with a couple other key projects I worked on*

Summary

This project challenged me for a couple of reasons. Not only had I never made a locket before, I had also never used silver solder. A new technique plus a new topic make for a very fun project!

Building a Brass-Ringed Mallet

I got a really great piece of 2"-thick white oak from a sawmill in Woodstock, New York. It had been drying for a long time, but was finally ready to be put to work. I used it to create a mallet with a brass-edged head. You can see the finished project in Figure 7-31.

The mallet isn't to pound nails or other metal objects. At the same time, it's also not for pounding wood, as the brass rings that reinforce the mallet head could ding the material. I'm mostly going to use it for mortising and for hitting the backs of chisels.

Figure 7-31 *I made this mallet out of white oak and brass*

Tools and Materials

I used the following tools and materials to make my mallet:

- Band saw
- Briwax clear wood polish
- Caliper
- Chop saw
- Planer
- Lathe
- Scotch-Brite pad
- Screw clamps
- Shoulder plane
- Table saw
- Titebond glue
- White oak

Building the Mallet

To create my mallet I followed these steps:

1. Cut off the handle portion

The first thing I did was cut a 1" strip off of one side of the board. This will be the mallet's handle, and ultimately I'm going to round it in the lathe to make it grip easier. For now, however, I'm going to set it aside and work on the head portion for awhile.

2. Smooth the wood

The white oak's surface still had band saw marks on it that I needed to remove, so I ran the remainder of the board through the planer. I wanted the wood as smooth as possible, because I would be gluing it together.

3. Cut up the board

There was a twist in the wood, so I played it safe and cut it halfway through—I was afraid the wood would bind if I made a full-depth cut, so I only cut halfway through, flipped over the board, then cut the rest of the way. I cut off two short sections on the chop saw to serve as the head.

4. Shape the handle

I grabbed the 1" piece of wood I'd cut off the edge of the board. This will be the mallet's handle. I drew the shape of the handle on the wood, working from memory to re-create a mallet handle I'd used in the past. It won't be glued, nailed, or anything else—it holds onto the head through a tapering of the wood, seen in Figure 7-32. Having drawn the shape of the handle on the strip of wood, I cut it out using my band saw.

Figure 7-32 *Cutting out the handle*

5. Cut and glue the head

I wanted to ensure that the handle fit snugly, so once I finalized its shape, I worked on the socket in the mallet's head. I drew a rectangle (seen in Figure 7-33) on the twin pieces of wood that make up the mallet head.

Figure 7-33 *Drawing the hole for the mallet handle*

I cut out the shape using the table saw, making multiple small cuts with the help of the saw's sled in order to make a precise hole for the handle.

Once the channel was cut, I needed to modify it to make it match the taper of the handle. I drew cut lines on the wood, then brought it back to the table saw.

I re-cut the hole, but this time at an angle to capture the negative of the handle's wedge shape. I used a chunk of wood to angle the blocks of white oak so that the blade's cut matches the taper I'd drawn on the wood.

It was a somewhat painstaking process because the angles have to be even or the handle won't fit or will be angled oddly. I used the cut line on the sled as a guide for getting the angle right. After I'd cut one channel, I made a test fit and then cut the other one.

I used a shoulder plane to smooth out the inside of the groove, then glued the head together using Titebond wood glue (Figure 7-34) and clamped it.

Figure 7-34 *Gluing the halves of the mallet head*

6. Shape the handle on the lathe

While the head's glue was drying, I put the handle in the lathe and went to work with a chisel. I wasn't trying to make a perfectly circular handle; I just wanted to round the edges. After I had shaped it the way I wanted it, I sanded it and did a test fit with the now-dried head.

7. Shape the head

I found the center of the end and used a compass to make a circle. It's possible to use the lathe to make a block into a circle, but I find cutting off the corners saves a lot of time.

Next, I set my band saw for 45 degrees and roughed out the corners, making my job with the lathe easier—smoothing out a cube of wood is a lot of work, and really noisy as well!

Then I put the head in the lathe (Figure 7-35) and worked on it with the chisel. It's very deceiving because it looks perfect when the lathe is spinning! Of course, you get a more accurate picture once the lathe has stopped, so I kept checking it.

One area that concerned me was that the hole in the head was chipping out when the chisel hit it, so I added some crazy glue around the edges to reinforce it. The glue keeps the fibers in place.

Figure 7-35 *Smoothing the mallet head on the lathe*

When I started getting the head where I wanted it, I cut into the ends, because ultimately I want to attach brass rings to the ends to reinforce them. The outer diameter of the brass pipe I'm using is three inches, so I kept the wood a hair over; I could always take it in if it was too wide. I played it safe and took a little bit off, then checked with my caliper to ensure I wasn't going too far.

I gave the head almost a football shape, tapered in at the ends. It's mostly for aesthetics, but it also accommodates the fact that my brass rings are three inches in diameter. Figure 7-36 shows the hammer's shape. Finally, I sanded the head with the pad from a disc sander while it spun on the lathe.

Figure 7-36 *The head takes on a "football" shape*

8. Add the brass rings

With the wood portion of the project done, I worked on the brass rings. I cut off 1" sections of brass pipe using my portable band saw.

Next, I cleaned up the rings in the belt sander. I hadn't made the effort to ensure the cuts I made were straight, so I held the brass rings firmly against the table of the saw so they would sand evenly.

When I milled the ends of the hammer, I tapered them somewhat so the rings would go on readily at first, but would need to be pounded into place to make them fully flush. While I was at it, I made a chamfer (a sloping surface) on each ring to help it fit onto the head.

I inserted the handle, which stays on with friction only. Holding the mallet by the handle, I tapped the rings into place. You can see me at work in Figure 7-37. I went slow, not wanting to damage the brass or oak.

When I had the rings pounded in as much as they would go, I brought the mallet to the belt sander and polished off the ends of the brass rings. While I was at it, I rounded the end of the handle sticking out.

Figure 7-37 *Tapping the brass into place*

9. Finish the mallet

I used a Scotch-Brite on the rings and Briwax to seal the wood. The mallet is done! I'm really proud of how it turned out.

Summary

One of the best reasons to make a tool is so you have it to use in the future. I can't wait to use my mallet in a future project. Now, build yourself one!

Mass-Producing a Signature Ice Pick

An ice pick is simply one of the tools I carry on my person. It's good for touching or moving something hot or sticky, things you don't want to touch with your hand. The project consists of a commercial ice pick with a replacement brass handle and protective sheath that lets you keep it in your pocket. You can see several of the picks in Figure 7-38.

For a long time I encouraged people to make their own, and people suggested I presell a batch of ice picks. I did, and sold over 100 of them, and that encouraged me to make more batches. Right now I'm sitting at over 1,000 ice picks manufactured. Follow along to see how I made them.

Figure 7-38 *I didn't just make an ice pick, I made hundreds of them*

Tools and Materials

The parts list for this project included the following:

- Band saw
- Box cutter
- Brass stock: hexagonal and tubular
- Brass ring
- Cyanoacrelate (a.k.a. "crazy") glue
- Lathe
- Propane torch
- Shopbot CNC router with a V bit

- Silver solder
- 3-in-One cutting oil
- Ultra Flux
- Vise

Building the Ice Picks

The actual process of creating the ice picks is relatively brief, but it seems much longer when you consider I built over 100 of them in the following steps:

1. Remove handle from ice pick

I began by placing each ice pick in the jaws of my vise and yanking off the wooden handle. I dumped the handles and kept the picks.

2. Cut the hexagonal stock

I cut the handles out of 3/8″ hexagonal brass stock, purchased from onlinemetals.com. Figure 7-39 shows me cutting the stock on the band saw.

Figure 7-39 *Cutting handles out of brass stock*

3. Engrave the handle

I set up a jig on my ShopBot CNC router, attached a V bit, and engraved my logo into every one of those handles.

4. Drill the handle

I put each length of hexagonal stock in my 16″ lathe and drilled one end with a 1/8″ bit. I made sure to use cutting oil because I was going to be making a lot of handles.

5. Taper the ends of the handle

I pencil-pointed both ends of the handle (Figure 7-40) with the lathe's cutting tool. The tapers will help give the ice pick a finished look.

Figure 7-40 *I tapered both ends of each handle*

6. Cut the brass tubing

The business end of the pick is protected with a brass "sheath" consisting of a length of tubing. I cut a bunch of lengths of tubing on the band saw.

7. Cut notches in the tubes

I used my Grizzly milling machine with a 1/8" mandrel bit to cut precise notches (seen in Figure 7-41) in the sheaths. These notches will accommodate brass rings.

Figure 7-41 *Using a mandrel bit to cut a rounded notch in the end of each sheath*

8. Solder on a ring

I placed the notched tubing on a special rig I welded together (seen in Figure 7-42) with a brass ring crimped into the notch. Then I dabbed some Ultra Flux and set a piece of silver solder on the join. When it was ready, I melted the solder with a pair of propane torches, and the melted silver fell into the crack. For future production runs I did away with the metal rig because it soaked up too much heat.

The final step to the soldering process involves quenching the join in a solution that clears away the excess flux before it adheres to the surface.

Figure 7-42 *Soldering on the rings*

9. Glue in the picks

I dipped the non-pointy ends of the picks into CA (cyanoacrelate or "crazy") glue and inserted them into the handles.People are surprised to see me use CA glue for this purpose. I do this for a very specific reason. If you use the pick, you might break the tip off. Just go buy another ice pick, heat the handle up and remove the broken part, then crazy-glue in the new part. Then I put each pick in my hand drill and polished off any excess glue using a razor blade and Scotch-Brite pad.

10. Add the dimple

I had an idea for securing the sheath to the handle, and it involves a dimple. With a hammer and tap, I made a small dent in the sheath. The dimple creates friction that keeps the sheath in place.

11. Cut the sheaths

First I set up a small saw blade on my lathe, and then I split the ends of the sheaths so that the slot runs perpendicular to the dimple. When I was done I buffed the cut ends smooth.

12. They're done!

I put the sheaths on the picks (Figure 7-43) and got ready to send them off.

Figure 7-43 *The completed ice picks ready to mail*

Summary

This project presented a new challenge to me: I wanted to manufacture and sell a product. I'd love for you to build your own version of this project. However, if you'd rather get one of these, I sell them at *http://shop.jimmydiresta.com*.

Grinding My Own Kris Knife

This knife (seen in Figure 7-44) is really the first one I ever made from scratch. I decided to make the most complicated shape the first time out because it can only get easier from there! I made a wavy-bladed knife, often called a kris- or Indonesian-style blade.

The knife was an ambitious project and I went in thinking it would be easy to complete, but it became one of those projects that started to linger. I kept thinking, "Ugh, I have to go back and work on that knife" and ultimately I set it aside for six months. When I purchased a metalworking forge and was able to heat-treat the steel properly, I picked the project back up and finished it. I'm really proud of how it turned out.

Figure 7-44 *I challenged myself by building a complicated design: a kris knife*

Tools and Materials

As you might imagine, most of the tools I used in this project involved grinding and polishing the metal:

- Beaumont sander
- Table saw
- Rigid milling machine
- Band saw
- Hand files
- Grinder with a 8" disk
- Pneumatic die grinder with a Scotch-Brite disk
- Burbinga wood
- Brass stock
- Five-minute epoxy
- 3/16" × 1.5" piece of steel
- 3M #77 spray adhesive

Creating the Knife

I followed these steps to make my knife:

1. Apply the design

I sketched out the design a few times before I made one I liked. Then I sprayed down a piece of A-2 steel, 3/16" thick by 1.5" wide, with some 3M #77 spray adhesive and stuck my design to the metal. Figure 7-45 shows me applying the design.

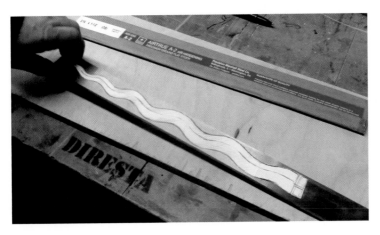

Figure 7-45 *Gluing the design to the steel stock*

2. Grind out the blade

I tried a couple of different ways to cut out my design, beginning with a band saw and jeweler's saw. I eventually figured out the easiest way would be to literally grind the excess material away, as seen in Figure 7-46. I have this crazy 8" grinding disk that literally turns the blade's negative space into dust. It's incredibly noisy and I'm wearing ear protection, as well as a dust mask and a protective face shield.

As always, I kept the paper design on the steel as long as possible, and as long as I stayed outside the line I was happy.

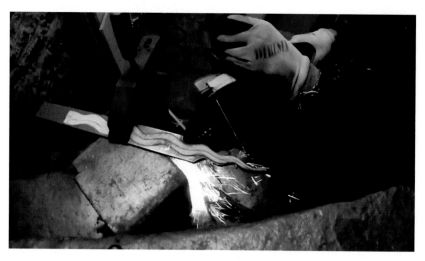

Figure 7-46 *Grinding the wavy shape out of a piece of steel*

3. Clean up the curves

The next thing I did was to sand down the knife's curves using my Beaumont belt sander, which was designed for knife making. I wanted the edge to be as smooth and consistent as possible, because if the pattern of curves was off, the eye would spot it immediately.

4. Bevel the blade

I drew a line bisecting the edge of the blade so I could see where the future edge would be. I wanted a double bevel, where the blade narrows evenly from both sides. I also wanted a center line along the flats of the blade, sort of a ridge mirroring the curves of the blade.

Then I went to work using an electric die grinder with a burr attachment. You can see me working in Figure 7-47. That burr is super strong and carves that metal right away. I would periodically draw in Sharpie on the part I wanted to grind, so that I could gauge my progress. After I had finished one side, I flipped it over and redrew the center line, and kept grinding.

Figure 7-47 *Grinding away at the metal*

5. File the blade

After I had ground away a bunch of material I brought the knife back to the Beaumont. Unfortunately it wasn't as much of a help as I thought it would be—I simply wasn't getting the results I was expecting because it was harder to see what I was grinding. It was easier to work on it with a hand file (Figure 7-48) because I could see what I was doing. It took days and days of work to get the blade shaped the way I wanted it.

Figure 7-48 *Working with hand files to finish the blade*

6. Polish the steel

When I was finally done shaping the steel, I polished it up with a pneumatic die grinder and a Scotch-Brite disk.

7. Heat-treat the blade

I heated up the blade in my propane furnace (seen in Figure 7-49) and when it was nice and red-hot, I left it out to cool. The kind of steel I used (A-2) belongs to a category of alloys called air-hardening steel, and part of the tempering process involves heating up the metal to upwards of 1700 degrees F, then letting it air-cool. After it had cooled I put it in my oven at 400 degrees to complete the tempering process.

Figure 7-49 *Tempering the steel*

8. Cut wood for the case

I was originally going to put the blade inside a cane, but during the six months when this project was quiescent, I decided it was just too fat. Instead I made a case that wasn't shaped like the blade—it would be totally rectangular.

I cut three strips of bubinga wood on my table saw, each big enough to fit the entire blade. The strips will form the case, with the center one cut to accommodate the blade.

9. Glue the case

I used Titebond wood glue, and secured everything with brad nails and a whole bunch of clamps. I attached just two of the three layers at first, then added the final layer once the first two were set.

10. Sharpen the blade

While the case was drying, I went back to the Beaumont and worked on sharpening up the edge. I really wanted to shave with the knife, but unfortunately I just couldn't get it sharp enough. While I was at it, I polished up the blade again with my die grinder. When I heat-treated the blade, it had been scorched black, and I polished off the soot.

11. Drill the tang

The part of the knife under the handle is called the tang. I drilled four holes in my knife's tang (Figure 7-50). I'll epoxy the handle on, and the holes are just there to give the glue something to grab ahold of.

Figure 7-50 *I drilled some holes in the knife's tang to give the glue a little extra gripping power*

12. Machine the guard

There is a little piece of metal that caps the handle as it meets the blade, called the guard. I used my Bridgeport mill to grind out the footprint of the blade, then cleaned it up on the Beaumont.

13. Cut apart the case

You've probably noticed the hilt and case are all in one piece; this is because I wanted the two parts to fit together relatively seamlessly. However, it was time to cut them apart on the band saw.

14. Epoxy the knife

I mixed up some five-minute epoxy and inserted the tang onto the blade, then slid it down until it was snug against the hilt.

15. Finish

I brought the knife to my Beaumont again and sanded down the edges of the case and hilt, including the part where the brass guard extends over the wood—I wanted them to be flush. I kept it slow so the epoxy wouldn't heat up and loosen. Finally, I rubbed the case down with boiled linseed oil. Figure 7-51 shows the completed kris knife.

Figure 7-51 *My finished knife, looking good!*

Summary

Considering how many months it took to make the kris knife, I'm really pleased with how it turned out. Finishing my first ever knife, and one with a difficult design, gave me a lot of confidence for future projects.

You've also reached the end of the book! Throughout this book I've shared my passion and knowledge of tools and materials, and I hope you find inspiration in these pages. Good luck with your next project!

Index

About the Authors

John Baichtal has written or edited over a dozen books, including the award-winning *Cult of Lego* (No Starch Press, 2011), LEGO hacker bible *Make: LEGO and Arduino Projects* (Maker Media, 2012) with Adam Wolf and Matthew Beckler, *Robot Builder* (Que, 2014), *Maker Pro* (Maker Media 2014), and *Hacking Your LEGO Mindstorms EV3 Kit* (Que, 2015). He's hard at work on his latest project, a compilation of LED projects for No Starch Press. John lives in Minneapolis with his wife and three children.

Jimmy DiResta is a designer and master maker known for his ability to artfully fabricate in an impressive range of materials. He has starred on a number of cable DIY shows, including *Hammered with John & Jimmy DiResta* (HGTV), *Trash to Cash* (FX Network), and *Dirty Money* (Discovery). Jimmy is currently a well-known maker star on YouTube where he creates regular videos for Make:, Core77, and his own popular and influential DiResta channel.

Colophon

The cover image is from David Waelder. The cover and body font is Myriad Pro; the heading font is Benton Sans; and the code font is Ubuntu Mono.

NOV 1 2015

NOV   2016